14 ⁹⁰

DATE DUE

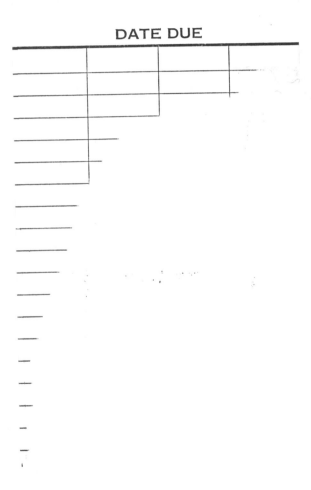

SPORTS

by Allen F. Richardson

Series developed by Peggy Schmidt

Peterson's

Princeton, New Jersey

A New Century Communications Book

Other titles in
this series include:

CARS
COMPUTERS
EMERGENCIES
FASHION
FITNESS
HEALTH CARE
KIDS
MUSIC
TRAVEL

Library of Congress Cataloging-in-Publication Data

Richardson, Allen F.,
   Sports / by Allen F. Richardson.
     p.   cm.—(Careers without college)
   "A new century communications book."
   ISBN 1-56079-250-7 : $7.95
   1. Sports—Vocational guidance—United States.   I. Title
  II. Series.
  GV583.R5   1993
    796' .023—dc20

93-4488
CIP

Art Director: Linda Huber
Cover photo: Bryce Flynn Photography
Cover and interior design: Greg Wozney Design, Inc.
Composition: Bookworks Plus
Printed in the United States of America
10 9 8 7 6 5 4 3 2 1

Text Photo Credits
Color photo graphics: J. Gerard Smith Photography
Page xvi: © Woodfin Camp & Associates, Inc./Gerd Ludwig
Page 18: © The Stock Market/Brian Peterson
Page 36: © Photo Edit/Tony Freeman
Page 54: © The Stock Market/Lewis Portnoy
Page 72: © Photo Edit/Michael Newman

ABOUT THIS SERIES

Careers without College is designed to help those who don't have a four-year college degree (and don't plan on getting one any time soon) find a career that fits their interests, talents and personality. It's for you if you're about to choose your career—or if you're planning to change careers and don't want to invest a lot of time or money in more education or training, at least not right at the start.

Some of the jobs featured do require an associate degree; others only require on-the-job training that may take a year, some months or only a few weeks. In today's increasingly competitive job market, you may want to eventually consider getting a two- or maybe a four-year college degree in order to move up in a field.

Each title in the series features five jobs in a particular industry or career area. Some of them are "ordinary," others are glamorous. The competition to get into certain featured occupations is intense; as a balance, we have selected jobs under the same career umbrella that are easier to enter. Some of the other job opportunities within each field will be featured in future titles in this series.

Careers without College has up-to-date information that comes from extensive interviews with experts in each field. The format of each book is designed for easy reading. Plus, each book gives you something unique: an insider's look at the featured jobs through interviews with people who work in them now.

We invite your comments about the series, which will help us with future titles. Please send your correspondence to: Careers without College, c/o Peterson's Guides, Inc., P.O. Box 2123, Princeton, NJ 08543-2123.

Peggy Schmidt has written about education and careers for 20 years. She is author of Peterson's best-selling *The 90-Minute Resume.*

ACKNOWLEDGMENTS

Special thanks to the following people who lent their time and expertise:

Pete Abitante, Director of Information, National Football League, New York, New York

Frank Ackley, Tennis Pro and Owner, Hither Hills Tennis Club, Montauk, New York

Vic Braden, Founder and Director, The Vic Braden Tennis College, Coto de Caza, California

Gayden Copper, Communications/Public Relations, United States Professional Tennis Association, Houston, Texas

Brad Danforth, Manufacturer's Representative, Danco, Oradell, New Jersey

Bob DiBiasio, Vice President of Public Relations, Cleveland Indians, Cleveland, Ohio

Bruce R. Dworshak, Director of Media Relations, Host Committee, Super Bowl XXVII, Los Angeles, California

Jon Eisen, PGA Golf Professional, South Fork Country Club, Amagansett, New York

Betsy Eggert, Freelance Boxing Photographer, Boston, Massachusetts

Jack Gallagher, Public Relations, London Monarchs, World League, London, England

Georgia Gibson, Executive Vice President, Manufacturers' Agents Association, Laguna Hills, California

Pat Greenhouse, Staff Photographer, *Boston Globe,* Boston, Massachusetts

Lois Halinton, Executive Director, Sporting Goods Agents Association, Morton Grove, Illinois

Martha Hassell, Academic Director, New England School of Photography, Boston, Massachusetts

Bob Hillman, Director of Public Relations, Arena Football League, Des Plaines, Illinois

Michael Huyghue, Vice President and Legal Counsel, Detroit Lions, Detroit, Michigan

Rusty Kasmiersky, Director of Media Relations, New Orleans Saints, New Orleans, Louisiana

John Kelly, Photojournalist and Instructor, Orange Coast College, Costa Mesa, California

Janet Knott, Photojournalist, *Boston Globe,* Boston, Massachusetts

Susan Lambeth, Freelance Rodeo Photographer, Archdale, North Carolina

Edwin W. Lawrence, Executive Director, Baseball Office for Umpire Development, St. Petersburg, Florida

Julius Mason, Director of Public Relations and Media Relations, Professional Golfers Association of America, Palm Beach Gardens, Florida

Ted Monica, General Manager, Power Athletic Equipment by Riddell, Houston, Texas

Edward H. McDaniel, PGA Golf Professional, The VIP Golf School, Columbia, Missouri

Mary Messenger, Freelance Sports Photographer, Rancho Cordova, California

Linda Navlyt, Equipment Manager, Horizon High School, Scottsdale, Arizona

John Okolovich, Director, Killington Ski School, Killington, Vermont

Ron Ohringer, Equipment Manager, University of Maryland, College Park, Maryland

Mark Rudolph, Officiating Program Director, USA Hockey, Colorado Springs, Colorado

Joe Sharp, Equipment Manager, Bowling Green State University, Bowling Green, Ohio

Kevin Smith, PGA Golf Professional, Montauk Downs Golf Course, Montauk, New York

Barry Stout, Director of Tennis, Killington Ski School, Killington, Vermont

Jon P. Stevenson, President, Association of Volleyball Professionals, Culver City, California

Rod Thorn, Vice President of Operations, National Basketball Association, New York, New York

Bill Topp, Assistant Editor, *Referee*, Referee Enterprises, Inc., Racine, Wisconsin

Jerome R. Vainisi, Vice President of Football Management, The World League, Dallas, Texas

James E. Wilkenson, Director of Development/Student Affairs, San Diego Golf Academy, Rancho Santa Fe, California

Kathy Willens, Sports Photographer, Associated Press, New York, New York

Starlin Ann Wood, High School Basketball Referee, Apache, Oklahoma

Bubba Withington, Manufacturer's Representative, Withington and Associates Agency, Atlanta, Georgia

WHAT'S IN THIS BOOK?

WHY THESE SPORTS CAREERS?

The multibillion-dollar sports industry and its superstars dominate the entertainment landscape of America. Michael Jordan, Nolan Ryan and Monica Seles are as likely to be on the cover of *Time* or *Newsweek* as a film star, a president or a rock idol. People wear the pricey sneakers their heroes endorse. Fans mob stadium exits for autographs.

A career in the world of sports can be the stuff of dreams, provided you are determined, willing to start at the bottom and available to work unconventional hours. While many in the sports world do have degrees, there are also jobs that don't require a four-year college education. They include:

❏ Club pro/instructor

❏ Sports official

❏ Equipment manager

❏ Sports photographer/videographer

❏ Manufacturer's representative

Still, there is plenty of competition for these jobs. To get in you need to be a quick study, want the job a little bit more than the next person and have the confidence to stick with it until you get the break you're looking for.

Club pros and instructors all have talent and skill in their sport—which they spend years perfecting—plus the ability to teach others how to play the game. Golf and tennis pros often get their experience by serving unofficial apprenticeships at local clubs, where they help with whatever chore needs doing, such as picking up golf balls at the range or feeding tennis balls into a machine. Many get training at a community college, a specialized sports school or a clinic run by professional organizations in their sport.

Sports officials also learn by doing. Baseball umpires usually make their first calls at Little League games; hockey officials train in Mite leagues; basketball referees debut in elementary school and pickup games. Join your local organization, read a rule book, pick up a whistle and get into the action as early as you can.

Equipment managers are now a vital part of sports, from the local high school to the Dallas Cowboys. They know about helmets, pads and balls and how to maintain them and, most importantly, how to keep the athletes who use the equipment safe from injury. Volunteer at your high school. You may do nothing more than launder uniforms and hand out towels in the locker room, but you can gain experience and knowledge by looking over your boss's shoulder and making yourself indispensable.

Sports photographers and videographers live in a world of glamour, but they sweat bullets to get the pictures that delight, amuse and even shock us: a triumphant Muhammad Ali standing over a decked Sonny Liston, or the weeping and injured sprinter Derek Redmond as his father helped him hobble over the finish line at the 1992 Summer Olympics. They develop their skill by shooting rolls of film of local sports events, perhaps for no pay or for just enough to cover their expenses. But as they get better, they can land staff jobs and often command good salaries.

Manufacturer's representatives are the people who sell sporting goods, apparel and footwear to the stores and pro shops where you shop. They also equip every team. You can get the sales experience you need by working for a retail sporting goods store. Learn about the products and who manufactures them and get to know the reps who visit your store.

Despite the keen competition for jobs, the sports industry continues to expand, creating more jobs. The National Hockey League will add four teams in the 1990s; Major League Baseball, two. The National Football League is also expanding, and soccer continues to grow. Money is finally pouring into women's college sports. And personal fitness continues to boom.

So pick your dream job and go for it.

REGGIE WILLIAMS

on Finding Your Place in the World of Sports

At 39, Reggie Williams is proof that there is life after football. A former National Football League star and team executive, Williams is also a dedicated social activist. Until June 1993 he was director of the NFL's Youth Education Town (YET), a community center in south central Los Angeles. He is now director of sports development for Walt Disney World.

Born in Flint, Michigan, where his parents were active in community service and civil rights, Williams learned early about the importance of hard work and study. His father toiled in a factory and drove a taxi. At night Williams did homework alongside both his parents, who were also earning high school diplomas.

Williams went to Dartmouth College, won a place on the football team and became an All-American. Drafted by the Cincinnati Bengals in 1976, he broke into the starting lineup as a rookie, then played right outside linebacker during every game of his 14-year career.

A star in two Super Bowls, he had a game-high ten tackles and one sack in Super Bowl XXIII against Joe Montana and the San Francisco 49ers. Williams retired from football in 1990 with 23 fumble recoveries, qualifying him for a third-place tie with legendary Minnesota Viking Carl Eller on the NFL's all-time record list.

Voted Bengals' Man of the Year from 1982 to 1986 for heroics on and off the field, Williams has dedicated his life to helping those with hearing and speech problems, both of which he overcame as a child.

In 1985 the NFL Players' Association gave him the prestigious Byron "Whizzer" White Humanitarian Award. In 1987 the Jaycees named him one of Ten Outstanding Young Americans, and he was honored by the National Council on Communicative Disorders.

Williams was the 1986 NFL Man of the Year and the 1988 *Sports Illustrated* Sportsman of the Year. In 1988 he was also appointed to the Cincinnati City Council, and he was later elected to a second term.

In 1991 Williams became general manager of the New York Knights in the NFL's World League. He hired the controversial run-and-shoot guru Darrel "Mouse" Davis as head coach and won a divisional championship in his first season.

Sports are full of incredible moments when all the pieces of your life fall together and connect. When I was growing up, Sunday afternoons were special because my father and I watched football games on television. Our favorite team was the Cleveland Browns.

Years later, when I was a rookie with the Bengals, we were in Cleveland for a crucial game. By coincidence, my father was in the stands. As I walked through the tunnel and saw the grass in that historic stadium, I thought about all the legendary guys who had gone there before me and how they had sweated and bled on that field.

I wasn't starting because the Bengals didn't have much confidence in me. But we were losing, and the coach threw me in. I played with real intensity because I was scared. We came back to win, and from then on I started.

Later there were more thrills, even in practice and on the bus and, of course, in winning the big games and sometimes even in losing them. That's the wonder of sports. There were tough times, too. I think of William Ernest Henley's poem "Invictus":

I thank whatever gods may be,
for my unconquerable soul.
I have not winced nor cried aloud;
under the bludgeoning of chance,
my head is bloodied but unbowed.
I am the master of my fate,
the captain of my soul.

That's my deal, although you don't think about a philosophy in the crunch—you just live it. My proudest moment came when I was introduced at Super Bowl XXIII in 1989: "Starting at right outside linebacker, Councilman Reggie Williams." My life in sports and my life in community service had converged.

I grew up never really expecting or planning to be a professional athlete. As a society we have an obsession with sports and put too much emphasis on professional sports and all that big money. That is too dangerous a carrot because the opportunities are too few.

I didn't mature physically or mentally until after high school. I've been hearing impaired from birth, but it wasn't discovered until the third grade. Anytime you are a little different from other kids the problems multiply. Because I couldn't hear sounds, I had problems repeating them, so I developed speech problems too. I learned to overcome them by focusing and reading lips. I can still get sloppy and miss things, especially if I don't concentrate and enunciate.

I made the freshman football team at college, but I had no inkling about the pros until I got a letter from the Bengals. My coach tore it up; he wanted me focused on the present. He was right.

When I was drafted, I just wanted to make the Bengals. Once I did, I didn't expect to play long. But I wanted to give something back, make a contribution to the community for the shot they had given me, so I got involved with the Cincinnati Speech and Hearing Center.

I believe that the most important thing you can learn is how to learn. I've always tried to build a parachute so if I think I'm going to crash or reach a dead end I have something to keep me going. That's also why I took on the job as general manager of the Knights in 1991. That meant leaving Cincinnati, which had become a comfort zone for me. The number one reason for leaving was my kids. I didn't want them to grow up under my shadow. But I also didn't want to always live off my former self. Notoriety can become a crutch. I threw the crutches away by leaving.

As a parent I'm interested in exposing my kids to as many different skills and sports as possible. Kids learn how to set goals and finish what they start if they get involved in sports. Young people today often miss the boat on that. An alarming number drop out of school. So if you really want to get the message to them, sometimes you must take the mountain to Mohammed rather than take Mohammed to the mountain.

That's what I had hoped to do with the NFL YET program. I had to pass that baton on to someone else, but I think I started the process of establishing a new, positive partnership in the south central Los Angeles area. An educational and recreation center has been built and will bring in NFL players involved in community work—the area has produced 109—for the benefit of at-risk youth.

We raised $2.5 million for the operating budget, enough to last at least five years. I think that's the strongest statement we could make to a community where people are used to others walking away from their problems.

With Disney I'm very excited about an opportunity to bring some magic to the world of sports. With its international reputation, Disney is in a unique position to take a leadership role. I'll head a new division in Orlando, and

I'll get to define a lot of what happens as we integrate sports into the company.

As a former general manager and player, I learned a lot about the jobs of people around me. Equipment managers are vital. They're skilled professionals, and safety is paramount to the job. There's nothing worse than when a player gets hurt and the equipment manager isn't prepared. We had a quarterback with the Knights who broke a rib, but the equipment manager had no rib pads. So the quarterback played hurt. Let's just say the equipment manager didn't get a bonus that day.

Nobody pats the refs on the back, even when they do a good job. A ref's job is like a policeman's—it has a certain down side. Doing your best is the only way to deal with the job. Players and coaches want accuracy and fairness. But a referee's biggest problem is the fans. We expect sportsmanship from athletes, but no one teaches fans that.

I also dealt with the manufacturer's reps. Theirs is a dog-eat-dog business. I'm not that demanding, really, but I do think they must provide service. There's no room for lemons, either in the product or the reps. Being a rep is a great way to get into sports—the job puts you in a locker room, and you're part of a team. I'm sure reps say, "They're using my football, they're wearing our helmets, my shoe made that cut."

I've been around sports photographers my whole career, and I have great admiration for how hard they work and how they capture that one moment of action. Sometimes that meant they were looking right up my nose. One of my hobbies is collecting photographs, especially sports photographs.

I've always been involved in team sports, but if a kid is thinking about a future sports career as a teaching pro and is interested in a specialized camp or school, I think the parents need to ask what that camp or school emphasizes. If it teaches winning at all costs, that's a problem. Kids need a competitive, nonhostile environment. You don't want youngsters feeling that their self-esteem is wrapped up in just winning. If, on the other hand, participation is what's emphasized, along with individual skills and teamwork, that's a positive.

FAMOUS BEGINNINGS

Charley Casserly, General Manager, Washington Redskins, National Football League

Casserly was 27 and a high school football coach in Massachusetts when he decided that he'd rather work in the NFL. So in 1977 he wrote to all 28 teams saying he would do anything, including mopping floors.

Washington Redskins coach George Allen offered him an intern job with no promises and no salary, and Casserly accepted. With $500 to his name and a dented 1969 Nova, he drove to Virginia and checked into an $8-a-night YMCA. He subsisted on peanut butter-and-jelly.

He started out fetching milk shakes for Allen and answered phones. But after eight months he was hired as a scout and later promoted to assistant general manager. In 1989, at age 40, he won the top job. In 1993, the Redskins won the Super Bowl with a roster Casserly had signed during typical 16-hour days. "Bulldog," as he's known, now drives a Volvo with no dents.

Cy Buynak, Equipment Manager, Cleveland Indians, Major League Baseball

Buynak is the dean of American League equipment managers, having served a total of 32 years with the Indians. Buynak started as a clubhouse helper, washing uniforms, cleaning shoes and picking up towels.

A typical day is now 15 hours during the season, but Buynak prefers that to the factory clock that once ran his life. Besides ordering and maintaining all the equipment for a major league team, Buynak does anything he can to help the players, including making sure their cars are washed and that their wives and mothers are picked up from airports.

Imagine getting paid to teach the sport you love while others have to content themselves with a little golf, tennis or skiing on weekends and vacations. That's the "work" of club professionals and instructors, who live out their dreams amid the posh surroundings of a club, resort or mountain. They may be someone else's employee, but when they are teaching they are their own boss.

Sports pros may teach individual clients or a group. A typical day might include lessons from dawn to dusk, teaching clients who are assigned to you if you're a rookie, or people you have known for years if you're an experienced pro. You might also pitch in on the phones or at the pro shop.

Success often depends on a pro's ability to first show clients how to be students again. Pros must also be good

1

listeners and analysts (of what their students are doing wrong) and be able to explain complex moves and skills in a simple, clear way. They have to be sensitive to different types of personalities and know how to offer feedback in a positive way. These teaching skills are just as important as knowing how to put topspin on a tennis ball or read the break on a green. Some people are born instructors—but most are made.

Club pros and instructors get a thrill out of seeing some-one else fall in love with the sport. When that happens, a client will keep coming back for more lessons, week after week or year after year, helping the pro earn his or her bread.

"I feel that everybody has a genius to play well," says tennis pro Vic Braden, a licensed psychologist who has spent 40 years teaching tennis and researching the scientific principles of the game. "Those of us who teach or coach have a lot to learn about how to access that genius. It's a privilege, not a right."

Many sports pros also have the opportunity to develop relationships with people they would not ordinarily meet. Knowing some of the movers and shakers may lead to a better job or even a different career. Or a pro might enjoy a less direct benefit: A lawyer who is a client might offer to handle a legal hassle for him at a reduced fee or for an extra set of lessons.

For those who are young and single, there is the added social advantage of meeting students of the opposite sex. This is one profession where business and pleasure can mix, usually without disastrous consequences.

When pros are not teaching, they may sell the equip-ment and apparel that goes along with their sport. Much of their income might depend on the profits of the pro shop. If you prove that you know how to run a successful one or that you're able to manage others, you may get promoted to managing a school of instruction or end up owning your own resort or club and have other pros work for you.

If you've taken lessons yourself and excel in a sport, this may be the career for you. You'll be playing the game you love and helping others do the same.

What You Need to Know

- ❑ Mechanics and rules of your sport
- ❑ The latest theories and trends in teaching the sport
- ❑ Equipment made for the sport
- ❑ Fashion trends in sports apparel and footwear

◆ **Getting into the Field**

Necessary Skills

- ❑ Ability to devise simple drills for beginners and more complex ones for advanced players
- ❑ Good communication skills
- ❑ Proficiency at your sport
- ❑ Ability to maintain and repair the equipment
- ❑ Good salesmanship (you'll probably also work in or manage the pro shop)
- ❑ Some computer know-how (to do budgets and keep inventory)

Do You Have What It Takes?

- ❑ An easygoing personality (to get along with clients and employers)
- ❑ Punctuality
- ❑ Patience
- ❑ Creativity in teaching (lessons must be tailored to a wide variety of people with different skills)
- ❑ Diplomacy and an ability to mediate (you may have difficult students or, in group classes, students who clash with others)
- ❑ Self-discipline to stay in shape and improve your game or skills

Physical Requirements

- ❑ Good personal hygiene and a neat appearance
- ❑ Good health and stamina

Education

A high school diploma is required for golf pros seeking PGA (Professional Golfers Association) certification. No formal education is required for tennis or ski instructors, though you may have to pass a skill test to get hired at a resort or club.

Licenses Required

None, but some clubs and resorts want their pros to be members of professional groups. Few golf clubs will hire a pro who is not a certified member of the PGA.

For tennis pros and ski instructors, certificates from professional groups are much less important. Tennis pros can get their badge of approval from the USPTA (United States Professional Tennis Association), which issues certification based on playing ability, skill in teaching and a written test on tennis and business knowledge.

Skiers may join the PSIA (Professional Ski Instructors Association), which oversees ratings for ski instructors and attempts to standardize teaching methods. The PSIA has five levels of certification, based on a pro's skiing ability and knowledge (as determined by written and demonstration tests).

Job Outlook

Competition for jobs: very competitive

For golf pros the competition is and will remain especially keen in the future. The PGA already has over 13,000 members and 9,256 apprentices. But turnover at the bottom is high, since most apprentices serve as assistant pros, with low pay and long hours. So getting in the door might be less difficult than landing a decent job once you qualify as a full-fledged PGA pro.

Projections for tennis pros and ski instructors are a little more optimistic, and turnover is higher, although both areas are also highly competitive. Because tennis is a less expensive and more accessible sport, tennis pros will find jobs more easily than ski instructors.

Entry-level jobs: assistant golf or tennis pro; junior ski instructor

Beginners

- ❑ Conduct or assist in teaching at tournaments and in classes and clinics
- ❑ Set up nets and ball machines (tennis)
- ❑ Give or assist other pros in individual lessons (for less money)
- ❑ Assist in pro shop sales
- ❑ Repair and maintain equipment
- ❑ Cover the phones (booking lessons, dealing with sales reps, handling complaints)

Head club pro, ski or tennis school manager

- ❑ Teach individual or group lessons
- ❑ Hire and train assistant pros or instructors
- ❑ Supervise lessons given by assistant pros or instructors
- ❑ Organize and supervise tournaments (tennis and golf); stage ski competitions or races
- ❑ Direct the activities of a school
- ❑ Do budgets, inventory and purchasing for pro shops and equipment rooms
- ❑ Supervise the work of maintenance crews

Tennis and golf pros generally work at least a six-day week during their season. Those who work in the Northeast and Midwest have shorter seasons—ranging from six to nine months—than their counterparts in the South and Southwest. Tennis pros can work year round if their facility has indoor courts.

Ski instructors may work every day during their short season, which can start as early as Thanksgiving and end as late as May, depending on the weather.

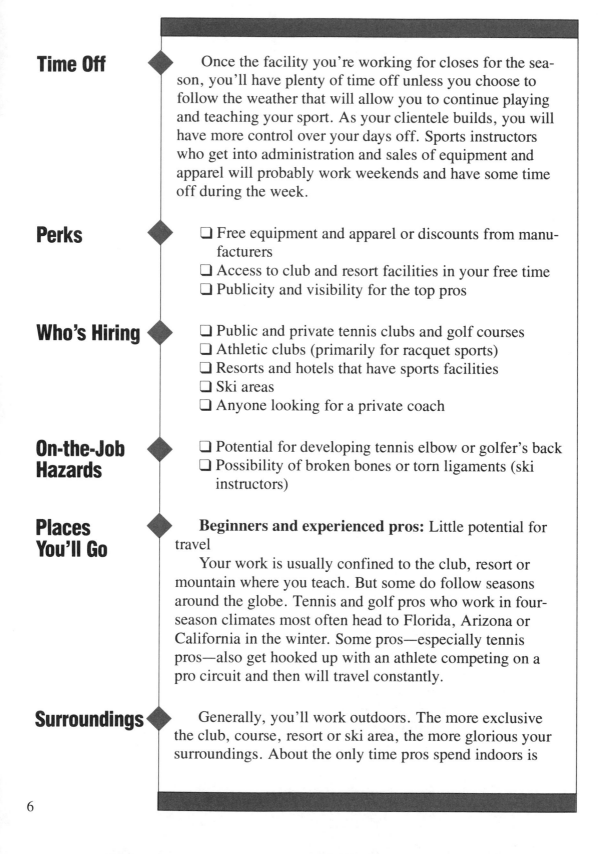

Time Off

Once the facility you're working for closes for the season, you'll have plenty of time off unless you choose to follow the weather that will allow you to continue playing and teaching your sport. As your clientele builds, you will have more control over your days off. Sports instructors who get into administration and sales of equipment and apparel will probably work weekends and have some time off during the week.

Perks

❑ Free equipment and apparel or discounts from manufacturers
❑ Access to club and resort facilities in your free time
❑ Publicity and visibility for the top pros

Who's Hiring

❑ Public and private tennis clubs and golf courses
❑ Athletic clubs (primarily for racquet sports)
❑ Resorts and hotels that have sports facilities
❑ Ski areas
❑ Anyone looking for a private coach

On-the-Job Hazards

❑ Potential for developing tennis elbow or golfer's back
❑ Possibility of broken bones or torn ligaments (ski instructors)

Places You'll Go

Beginners and experienced pros: Little potential for travel

Your work is usually confined to the club, resort or mountain where you teach. But some do follow seasons around the globe. Tennis and golf pros who work in four-season climates most often head to Florida, Arizona or California in the winter. Some pros—especially tennis pros—also get hooked up with an athlete competing on a pro circuit and then will travel constantly.

Surroundings

Generally, you'll work outdoors. The more exclusive the club, course, resort or ski area, the more glorious your surroundings. About the only time pros spend indoors is when they work in the pro shop, fix equipment or give indoor lessons (tennis mostly, but also golf in some big cities).

Dollars and Cents

Assistant golf pros might make $15,000 to $20,000 a year. Club pros will usually charge $30 to $60 an hour, with fees escalating to over $100 an hour. Famous golf gurus charge over $1,000 a day.

Tennis pros who rent teaching space from public courts or clubs will make only slightly more than their out-of-pocket expenses until they build up a clientele. Then they can make from $6,000 to $15,000 a year. A private club or resort may pay $17,000 to $35,000 a year. Celebrity tennis pros can command $75 an hour and earn $100,000 to $200,000 annually.

Ski instructors can start as low as $6 to $10 a hour and will often bartend or wait tables to supplement their income. Intermediate level instructors may make $20 to $55 an hour. Celebrity instructors can earn $250 to $350 a day.

Moving Up

Assistant golf pros move up to head pro or golf director either by staying at one facility or moving to another. The very lucky few buy a driving range or design their own golf course. Some even play their way onto the pro tour.

Tennis pros establish a reputation and then join better resorts for higher-paying jobs. They may then become directors of tennis schools, manage a tennis club, or become tournament supervisors. Some become tennis club owners.

Ski instructors are generally the most nomadic pros, although some start at the best ski areas and stay an entire career, building a name and a loyal clientele. These pros can also move to the front office, managing a ski school, or into general supervision of the entire resort.

Where the Jobs Are

An estimated 8,000 public golf courses and 1,000 resorts dot the U.S., but California, Arizona, Texas, Florida and the Carolinas have the heaviest concentrations.

Many tennis courts and clubs are affiliated with golf

clubs and resorts and so are also concentrated in states where the weather is good most of the year. But New England, New York, the Midwest and most of the mid-Atlantic states also have large numbers of both public and private courts.

Ski instructors can choose from over 700 ski areas in the U.S. and Canada, most of which are concentrated in New England, New York, Colorado, Utah and California.

Training

Numerous golf schools can help you develop playing and teaching skills, learn the business side of the profession and learn how to maintain equipment. Most offer job placement services for graduates. Programs run six months to two years.

The USPTA offers seminars, workshops, conventions and a continuing education program. Tennis pros can also polish their skills and earn further certifications at the Vic Braden Tennis College, the Van der Meer Tennis Center, the Nick Bollettieri Tennis Academy and other tennis schools.

Ski schools that are part of large ski resorts offer clinics in how to become an instructor. The PSIA also provides classes, seminars, workshops and clinics.

The Male/Female Equation

Tennis and skiing currently offer the most opportunities for women. However, approximately 80 percent of ski instructors are male, and about 70 percent of tennis pros are male. Golf is even more of a male-dominated sport, although more women are taking up the game.

The Bad News

❏ Long hours, low pay to start
❏ Jobs may not be full time
❏ A very competitive market
❏ Demanding or difficult clients

The Good News

❏ A certain amount of independence
❏ Outside work, usually in great surroundings
❏ Discounts on equipment and apparel
❏ Access to great facilities to play your sport

◆ **Making Your Decision: What to Consider**

◆ **More Information Please**

The Professional Golfers Association of America (PGA)
100 Avenue of the Champions, Box 109601
Palm Beach Gardens, Florida 33410
407-624-8570
Write for "Steps Toward PGA Membership," a brochure that details the PGA's extensive apprenticeship program. Or contact one of the 41 regional PGA offices.

United States Professional Tennis Association (USPTA)
One USTPA Center, 3535 Briarpark Drive,
Houston, Texas 77042
713-97-USPTA
Ask for "How to Apply for USPTA Membership," which describes the group's eight-hour certification training course.

Professional Ski Instructors of America (PSIA)
133 South Van Gordon Street, Suite 101
Lakewood, Colorado 80228
303-987-9390
Turn Pro explains how to apply for membership. PSIA offers clinics, workshops and educational tools. Members also get *Professional Skier* magazine and access to the *PSIA Accessories Catalog,* which offers discounts on equipment and apparel.

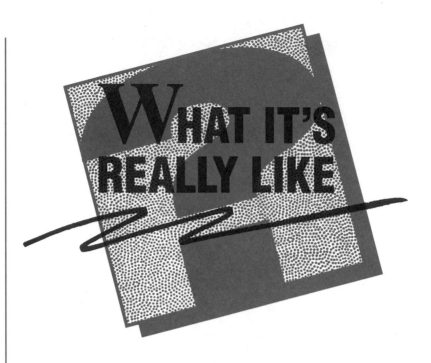

Leo Simonetta, 32,
golf professional,
Stonecreek Golf Club,
Paradise Valley, Arizona
Years in the field: two

When did you start playing golf?
I was about 14. From the first time I picked up a golf club
or watched golf on TV, I thought about playing on the pro
circuit. But by my late twenties I had played in many amateur tournaments. I finally knew that it would require more
effort and time than I had.

What were you doing then?
I was waiting tables at night in Las Vegas so I could play
or practice six days a week. But I wasn't thinking about
golf as a business or career. I was just coasting, making a
comfortable living and having fun. Then I finally decided I
had to get serious.

How did you get more training?
I went to the San Diego Golf Academy. I didn't go there
for my game; I went to learn about the business of golf.
It's an accelerated program [16 months] that gave me a

head start when I began my career. I went straight to Stonecreek as an assistant golf professional. I was dumbfounded when they offered me the job of acting head professional after only seven months.

How do aspiring pros usually get started?
They start in their teens as range pickers, picking up balls on a driving range. They work in the bag room (cleaning and repairing shoes and equipment). They work in the pro shop. And more pros go to school now, because golf is such a big business and you need some marketing background.

What are your current responsibilities?
I oversee the golf shop staff, a guest service staff of 12 and the range pickers. I'm also involved in the selling, organization and running of golf tournaments. We get phone calls from people who want to arrange a golf outing, and my responsibility is to get that business.

Do you teach?
I don't teach much here except at clinics. Most pros do teach a lot. But I took this job to learn more about the business. I already had teaching and playing experience.

What are the hours like?
I work 55 to 60 hours during a six-day week. I don't know if a five-day week exists in golf. Becoming a golf professional is hard work. But if you want to be successful, you accept that.

What's the worst thing about the job?
That I can't play golf more. But I knew that coming in, so for me it's not a negative. I do have a golf course right outside my office, so in the late afternoon I can put my shoes on and play nine holes. I don't know too many people who have that luxury.

What's best about the job?
The folks around golf are great, and you meet so many new people. Everyone who comes through the door is here to have fun, so it's a great working environment. It's fun to live out a dream. Sometimes I have to pinch myself.

What advice do you have for aspiring pros?
You have to enjoy people, love the game and be knowledge-able about it. You can lose the respect of members and guests very quickly if you don't know the answer to a rules question. Having a good game also helps. Members have more respect for pros who play well, especially if they teach. That establishes their credibility and fills the lesson book faster.

Leslie Cormier-Guth, 30,
ski instructor,
Killington Ski Area,
Killington, Vermont
Years in the field: 12

How did you become a ski instructor?
I started skiing when I was four or five at Powder Ridge, a tiny little hill in Connecticut. After high school I came up here with the intention of going to college, but I started teaching skiing instead.

I took the Killington instructor's course. It lasts five days and is very intense. I graduated and got a full-time job right away. You don't necessarily have to be an expert skier as long as you have people skills. They can always teach you to ski, but it's more difficult to teach someone how to teach.

Do you make a living teaching skiing?
Yes. I work from the first of November to April. From May to September I teach horseback riding, but skiing pays the rent.

Do most ski instructors work full time?
We have part-time instructors who just enjoy coming up on weekends to relax and teach. Some of them have high-powered jobs and don't need the money. Then you have the full-time instructors like me, who are doing this as a career. They teach 12 days on and 2 days off, usually Saturday and Sunday, when the part-timers and beginners fill in for us.

Describe a typical day.

At 8 A.M. we often have morning tech-talk, a class that I teach about the different techniques of skiing. At nine we have a lineup or ski-off. We watch the skiers come down and decide what groups to put them into. We use our system to rate them on their ability, from one to ten. Then we work with them throughout the day. We also have an accelerated program for beginners. They work their way up, gradually improving their technique or ability. They can go from beginner to even expert.

Do you give private lessons?

I can be booked all day. I have a good clientele that comes back every year. It develops gradually over the years and depends on how well you speak and sell yourself. You also have to sell the product, which is skiing.

Do you find teaching satisfying?

I mostly teach adults here, and I really like that. But people forget how to be students. It's a challenge to get them into that mind-set again. When was the last time someone told you to do something or that what you were doing was wrong? I'm the person who guides them through the process and helps them make that first breakthrough. Then everything falls into place.

What's the toughest part of your job?

Keeping up with changes in the industry; it evolves constantly, almost daily. You'd better know about the new equipment, the new clothing, the new lifts, the new snow-making guns.

You have to know it, but you have to teach others too. Take the clothing. In Vermont you have to dress right. Certain fabrics are better than others. It can get very cold here—I've skied when it's 30 degrees below. Protecting people from their own ignorance is part of the job. They also need education on safety and the inherent risks of skiing.

How do you keep your teaching skills up-to-date?

We have afternoon clinics every day in January, February and March. We get the instructors out with other instructors. Everyone has his or her own bag of tricks, so it's nice to find out what your peers know. Instructors are at different levels, too. We have some of the best in the country, some who are just starting and everything in between.

What's the best part about teaching skiing?
Being outside. And meeting people.

Do you get to ski much?
The clinics are all on the snow. We also compete with each other. We have a local ski-bum race on Wednesday. I enjoy a little friendly competition. And when I'm teaching, I always get to put in a few turns for myself. I also spend my weekends off skiing.

What's your proudest achievement?
Having people come back year after year. That's the best form of flattery, no matter what their level of skiing. It's also nice to hear they went out to dinner with their friends and talked about you.

What advice do you have for aspiring ski instructors?
They should take the instructor's course, which is open to the public. You're on the snow seven hours a day for five days. It doesn't guarantee a job, but it gets you in the door.

Roy Vazquez Jr., 24, head professional, the Vic Braden Tennis College, Coto de Caza, California
Years in the field: five

When did you first start playing tennis?
As a freshman in high school. My school didn't have a tennis team, but there was an annual tournament which I won as a sophomore and every year thereafter.

When did you first consider becoming a pro?
I was watching ESPN and saw a commercial about Tyler Junior College in Texas. It's a regular junior college, but you can get an associate degree in applied science with a major in tennis. We studied everything, such as coaching tennis in a team situation, club management and how to program a tennis club. We had a mental toughness class.

We learned how to string rackets. We also had 15 hours of lab a week, everything from lectures to watching teaching videos to doing on-court teaching.

Did you get any practical experience?
They require you to work at a summer tennis camp for five weeks. But I never did that because my parents were splitting up, so I went home and didn't finish the degree.

What happened next?
I worked in a store, taught tennis part time and coached basketball. I also worked at tennis summer camps. After about a year at home, I headed for California because I heard there were good opportunities there to become a pro.

What did you do out there?
I worked at a club that Tracy Austin's sister, Pamela, operated for several months. Then I got a job with a big tennis academy nearby. I started looking around for another spot when there were changes made at the academy.

I found out the Vic Braden College was nearby, so I went there. I had used Braden's books at Tyler, so getting to meet him was a big thing. It's not easy getting a job there, because you need to know his system. So I observed for a while and took notes. Before long a pro happened to leave and they offered me a job.

Do you support yourself now?
For a single person I'm making decent money. But I'm having problems because I've had some injuries and doctor's bills. Most people normally stay at Vic's place for about a year or two and learn what they can, then they leave because they're not making a lot of money.

Describe a typical day.
I come in at 8 A.M., unlock everything, set up all the ball machines and get the water ready. I assign the coaches to students. I also give private lessons after work some days.

Before we go on the court, we start the day with a classroom lecture. After that we break out into groups and start teaching. We have a video court where we tape students, then show them what's going on. That's a great teaching tool, especially if a person is a visual learner.

Describe the school's programs.
We have two-, three- and five-day programs for adults, and we're starting to do some juniors now, too. We've got everything from beginner level to open player level. The goal, no matter what the level they are at, is to make them improve as fast as they can.

Are you responsible for bookings or the pro shop?
I sometimes take reservations for the college. We have a pro shop, but someone else does that, and our manager does the budgets. I do about 80 to 90 percent of the stringing [of rackets] here.

What was hardest about getting established?
Finding work wasn't that easy, especially back East. There you have to be established in an indoor facility or you're not going to work because of the weather in the winter.

Right now I'm busting my tail working here, but it's a good spot. The money is just enough to get by, but the learning and research here is really going to help me in the long run.

What do you like most about your job?
Being outside; I spend about six hours of my nine-hour day in the sun. When I'm on court I'm happy as can be helping people out, seeing them change. And I get to meet people all the time. I met the girl that used to play Lori Beth on *Happy Days*. I just met the producer from *Home Improvement* and somebody who works on the lot for *Cheers*.

What do you like least?
The paperwork, the office work, phone calls.

Do you have an achievement you're proudest of?
Working here is a real honor. Having this job on my resume is the big time.

What advice would you give aspiring tennis pros?
Study the game. If you are going to school and you really want to learn about the mechanics of tennis, take classes that teach you about the human body and how it works.

Also go out and watch how different pros work. Always ask if something can be done better another way. Just because somebody says that's the way to do it doesn't mean it's right.

The game is on the line. A runner barrels into the catcher at home plate, spewing dust into your face. For a split second, time stands still as 60,000 spectators—and maybe millions more watching on TV—suddenly focus on you. You must make the call, safe or out, that could send one team to the World Series and the other home for a long winter.

I f that hot-seat role appeals to you, then the job of sports official may be your calling. Officials enforce the rules, set the clock and break up fights. They control the game and ensure that sports remain sportsmanlike. They are the civilizing influence and the last authority. But best of all, they are central to the action and inside the game.

That applies at every level, from junior hockey to the Stanley Cup, from recreational swimming to the Olympics. The drama and thrills are there for you to seize and help determine. Ask refs why they do what they do and they will reply: For the love of the sport.

But what does the person in the striped shirt get for what he or she gives to the game? Certainly not fame or fortune. Kids don't collect trading cards of umps and refs. Except at the highest levels of professional sports—Major League Baseball, the National Hockey League or the National Basketball Association—the pay is not great, and the job is strictly part time.

A successful official needs nerves of steel. You have to know the fine print in the rule book better than even those who make their living playing, coaching or writing about the game. No matter who says what, you have to trust your memory and judgment, stick to your guns and take the heat.

It's not that unusual for the ref to be right and everybody else wrong, whether it's on the professional golf tour at Augusta or at a Little League game in Hoboken, New Jersey. But even when you are right, you'll often be criticized, even berated.

Call an elementary school game and you might get the raspberries from parents or people you grew up with. Baseball managers will kick dirt on your feet when they don't like a call. Football coaches will scream at you from the sidelines, and your decision will be reviewed in slow motion for the television audience and projected on huge stadium screens for the fans in attendance.

Make a bad call—you're only human—and you still must stand your ground and take your medicine, which can be humiliating. But right or wrong, if you do the job well, you will eventually earn the respect of your peers and that of coaches, players and fans.

Officials get their real training on the job, usually starting as youngsters or teenagers, first playing the game and then officiating it. Later, most officials hone their skills at clinics and summer camps, where top pros offer instruction and simulate real game situations.

Getting a job as a referee is one of the easiest and quickest ways of getting in on the action. If you're a sports nut and happen to be the cool, calm, collected type, making tough calls may be just the spot for you.

What You Need to Know

❏ Rules of the game (including the fine print)
❏ Hand signals (or signs) that convey your rulings

Necessary Skills

❏ Quick reflexes and good coordination
❏ Good communication skills (for explanations to players and coaches; some refs discuss infractions with other refs before making a ruling)
❏ Personal budgeting skills (you might work for months on the road and need to budget your money and file an expense report)
❏ A decent command of Spanish in some sports, especially baseball

Do You Have What It Takes?

❏ Self-confidence, quick judgment and coolness
❏ Thick skin (to handle criticism)
❏ A sense of fair play (to interpret the rules, not just enforce them)
❏ Flexibility (to adapt the rule book to real game situations)
❏ A competitive spirit (the players are giving their all; so should you)
❏ A deep love of the game

Physical Requirements

❏ Stamina (for long games, long road trips and long seasons)
❏ Good athletic skills (depending on the sport, you may have to throw a baseball, toss up a basketball or skate well)

Education

A high school diploma is necessary to register with most officiating schools and governing organizations.

◆ **Getting into the Field**

Licenses Required

None for most children's sports such as Little League baseball and recreational sports, where sports officials work on a volunteer basis. But check with your local or state authorities.

High school officials need certification from their state or local association. Certification can involve passing a competency and rules test, attending clinics or camps and paying dues of between $15 and $50. Many refs and umps belong to local associations.

College officials are not regulated by a national or state certification process but usually belong to regional or conference associations, which provide training and a network of schools that hire officials on a seasonal or game-by-game basis. Hockey refs must register with USA Hockey, which is responsible for the testing and education of refs.

Those aspiring to the professional level of baseball, hockey or basketball must apply to the respective league. (Each hires and trains its own officials.)

Job Outlook

Competition for jobs: extremely competitive at the pro level; much more open at other levels

Major League Baseball has only 64 full-time umpires; the average number of job openings is usually one or two a year. Another 210 work in the minor leagues, where openings are more plentiful because of high turnover.

The NHL has 51 full-time professional refs and several hundred in the various minor leagues. The NBA has over 50 full-time professional refs and also trains refs in the officiating program of its feeder league, the Continental Basketball Association (which has 50 refs).

Job openings are more plentiful as you move down the ladder to part-time officiating in schools and colleges. Local amateur teams offer the best possibilities for a quick entry.

Beginners

❑ Umpire or officiate: recreational or elementary-level sports
❑ Junior high or high school sports
❑ Small college sports

◆ **The Ground Floor**

Experienced officials

Same as above, plus:
❑ Umpire or officiate: state high school tournaments
❑ College and university games and championship series
❑ Professional sports games and championship series

◆ **On-the-Job Responsibilities**

During the season for your sport, the hours are never nine to five, and weekends and holidays are usually spent on the job. Most junior leagues play during the day, while most high school sports and professional leagues play at night or on weekend afternoons.

Baseball runs from early spring to late fall. Basketball and hockey are played from early fall to late spring. Football is played from late summer to mid-winter.

◆ **When You'll Work**

For professionals, vacation time comes during the off-season of their sport. Most professional teams also take a day or two off during the week (basketball and hockey) or every other week (baseball). Days off are also governed by contracts between sports officials' unions and leagues.

During the off-season, most refs and umpires attend camps, clinics, seminars and conventions to network, brush up on skills and gain knowledge for moving up.

◆ **Time Off**

❑ Travel and lodging paid for (at the pro level)
❑ Free uniforms (sometimes)

◆ **Perks**

Who's Hiring

- ❏ Amateur sports leagues, clubs and organizations
- ❏ Recreation departments or any group that sponsors recreational leagues and tournaments
- ❏ Elementary, junior high and high schools, usually through local or state sports official associations
- ❏ Community colleges and universities, sometimes through conference associations
- ❏ Professional sports leagues (and associations)

On-the-Job Hazards

- ❏ Possibility of injury if you get caught up in the action
- ❏ Possibility of stress-related health problems

Places You'll Go

Beginners: little potential for travel
Experienced officials: moderate to extensive travel opportunities

Local travel is the norm. Those who officiate at the high school level may travel dozens of miles to a school for a game or hundreds of miles to state tournaments. College officials travel within a conference, which can involve travel to another state. The pros can clock well over 200,000 miles a year, traveling to most of the country's major metropolitan areas and making the occasional trip overseas for the Olympics or foreign exhibition games.

Surroundings

Officials work outside on playing areas ranging from dusty countryside baseball diamonds to state-of-the art Astroturfed stadiums. Inside, they may officiate in crowded school gymnasiums or high-tech dome structures. The one constant is the noise from screaming fans. The atmosphere is exciting, but it can be nerve-racking. This is no job for people who can't handle crowds.

Weather is also a major factor in some sports. Football is played no matter how bad the weather, and the game can last over three hours. A baseball game is usually suspended by rain, but the season starts in the early spring, when temperatures can be quite low, and ends in the late fall, when snow sometimes interrupts play.

Like the athletes and coaches, officials shower and change in the locker room, which can range from semi-luxurious to cramped and dank.

Dollars and Cents

Major League Baseball umpires earn annual salaries of $60,000 to $200,000, plus expenses. A World Series share can net $15,000. In the minors, pay is $1,700 to $3,100 a month. College baseball umpires make from $800 to over $1,000 for a championship series.

National Basketball Association (NBA) referees earn $51,000 to $152,000. The Continental Basketball Association (CBA) pays $125 to $175 a game.

Men's NCAA Division I basketball refs average about $366 per game; play-offs pay $500. Division II basketball refs make about $115 a game; Division III pays $91. Refs in Women's NCAA Division I basketball average $180 a game; in Divison II, $99; in Division III, $85. Basketball play-offs in Division I, II or III net fees from $175 to $275.

Refs in the National Football League are part time, with pay of $700 to $2,400 a game; play-offs pay $7,000. The Super Bowl pays $8,500. The Arena Football League (indoor pro football) pays $200 a game.

Officials in Division I college football earn an average of $350 a game. Division II pays $137 a game; Division III about $88. NCAA Division I-AA title and championship games pay refs $275; Division II, $225; Division III, $175. The NAIA pays $100 for a play-off game.

National Hockey League officials make $33,000 to $90,000 a year. The NHL's minor-league system—the International Hockey League (IHL) and American Hockey League (AHL)—pay $125 to $200 a game; linesmen are paid $65 to $90. The United States Hockey League, Junior A level, pays $150 a game; linesmen make $75. Division I college referees make about $300 a match; linesmen get $150. High school refs earn about $40 a game; linesmen earn $20. Junior club games pay $14; linesmen make $8.

College soccer refs make $130 for both men's and women's championship matches; linesmen get $80 a match. Junior soccer referees make $110 a game in boy's and girl's championship tournament play; linesmen make $78 a match.

Tennis officials earn about $600 for a major tournament such as the U.S. Open. A typical "volunteer" official works about ten tournaments a year to make approximately $5,000 before expenses (which can be significant).

Referees and umpires at the elementary, junior high and high school levels make $5 to $250 a game. When refs officiate recreational sports, they may earn a $5 to $10 fee for each game—or nothing.

(Figures change because of new labor agreements and readjustments in fee schedules by state and local associations, athletic conferences and school districts. Some figures here are courtesy of *Referee* magazine.)

Moving Up

Those who start officiating Little League games and junior hockey in their early teens can be working at the higher levels of minor league baseball and hockey or even in the big leagues in their twenties.

Those who don't get into officiating until later generally start officiating elementary school basketball, for example, and work their way up to high school and college hoop. The process can take years, if not decades. Some officials find a niche, such as junior varsity football, that they enjoy and stay there.

Where the Jobs Are

Many jobs are in your own backyard with the sports teams and leagues in your area. Local community colleges or universities are another option for those with experience. Professional sports teams are located in major metropolitan areas.

Training

Umpires can get training at a variety of camps and schools, usually held in late winter in Florida or Arizona.

Make sure they are sanctioned by Major League Baseball if professional work is your goal. Basketball camps and clinics are held all over the country, usually in the summer. Colleges and universities also offer courses and special camps for training refs.

USA Hockey trains its refs through seminars, camps and clinics. Anyone in this country seeking promotion to the National Hockey League's full-time professional ranks usually has to start at this level. (Canada, the real hotbed of hockey, has its own system.)

An estimated ten percent of all "amateur" officials (high school and college) are women, according to *Referee* magazine, the bible of sports officials. As of early 1993, no women worked as sports officials in professional baseball, basketball or ice hockey. However, USA Hockey estimates that 250 women referees (out of 11,000 total refs) are working at some level.

Sports in which women are making headway include high school and women's college basketball, volleyball, softball and soccer.

◆ **The Male/Female Equation**

The Bad News

❏ Low pay for beginners
❏ Constant pressure
❏ Only part-time work for most
❏ Possibility that fame may only come because you made a bad call
❏ Too much travel (especially for pros)

The Good News

❏ Being part of a sport you love
❏ Personal satisfaction when you make good calls
❏ The excitement of being in the thick of the action
❏ Good pay at the professional level
❏ You can tell your grandchildren Michael Jordan said, "Nice game, ref."

◆ **Making Your Decision: What to Consider**

More Information Please

Baseball Office for Umpire Development
P.O. Box A, 201 Bayshore Drive S.E.
St. Petersburg, Florida 33731
813-823-1286
Write for *Making the Call: Becoming a Professional Baseball Umpire,* which explains what you need to know and how to apply. A list of umpire training schools is also included.

USA Hockey
4965 North 30th Street
Colorado Springs, Colorado 80919
719-599-5500
USA Hockey is the national governing body for amateur ice hockey. Write or call for the brochure *Officiating Program,* which explains how to register with a local office and has information on educational materials, insurance, newsletters, rule books, clinics, camps and seminars.

National Basketball Association
Olympic Tower
645 Fifth Avenue
New York, New York 10022
212-826-7000
Write to this address or send a resume. You will receive information on how to apply.

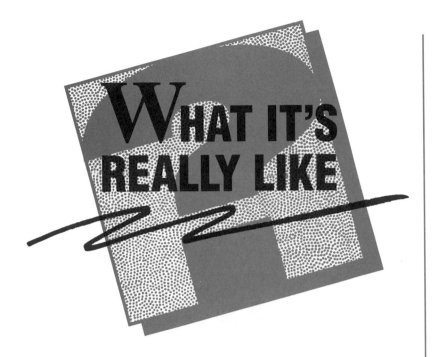

Chris Jarboe, 23,
baseball umpire, Southern League (AA),
Baltimore, Maryland
Years in the field: four

Did you play baseball as a kid?
I played all the time from the age of six or seven, and if I
couldn't find a game, I threw a ball against the wall. I
dreamed about playing professional ball but didn't take my
injuries seriously enough. I tried to play through them. I
dislocated my shoulder several times, I broke my collar-
bone, and I hurt everything else. After my junior year of
high school, I had to stop. I couldn't stand the pain anymore. My spikes are hung up forever.

When did you start umpiring?
In Little League, when I was 13. I got $10 or $15 a game,
and that was like a million bucks.

How did you progress from there?
I started hanging out at Towson State's baseball field [in
Baltimore]. One day I asked for work. I was 17, but I didn't
say anything about my experience. I was asked to do a dou-
bleheader. I thought it would be some low-level game, but

29

it was between Towson State and Long Island University. I was in shock. I guess I was hired because I looked very determined, and they were desperate because an umpire had canceled.

How did you do?

I was very nervous. I had put my nose in the rule book every now and then but never really concentrated on it like I do now. Billy Hunter, a former [Baltimore] Orioles player, was managing Towson. I was in awe just being on the same field with him. In the first game, I made a call and Hunter came charging out of the dugout to argue. I thought he was going to eat me for lunch. He started yelling and scream-ing. But I stood my ground.

How about the second game?

I was even more nervous. I got ridiculed by players. They didn't like my strike zone, which was textbook. I had a pretty good grasp of what a ball and a strike were but only to pitchers and batters in Little League.

When did you decide to become a full-fledged umpire?

I was going to community college, but when baseball sea-son came around I started ditching classes. At home I dab-bled in the rule book instead of school books and practiced my strike calls in the mirror. It became an obsession. I finally quit college. Tuition for umpire school was $1,700, and my dad took out a loan. He was skeptical, but I was determined to prove myself to him.

How does umpire school help?

It's taught by major and minor-league guys, so you're get-ting instruction from people in the system. If you can do the job, you've got a real shot at a position. I graduated among the top 25 percent, so they sent me to a nine-day camp with the top 48 prospects in the country. There they increase the intensity and see how you react in real playing situations. I was among 14 assigned to spring training.

What did you do?

Rookie ball, where younger players and umpires try to prove themselves and sharpen their skills. The crew chief (a senior umpire) helps you develop a style that will appeal to supervisors later on.

That June I got a contract for $1,700 a month and $30 a day for meals and lodging. The season ended in August, but I did well and got assigned to instructional ball for the fall. We made $55 a day but had to pay for expenses. So I made absolutely no money. But I wasn't there to make money.

And the next season?
I got the Midwest League—A-ball and a 142-game season. I got $100 more, just enough to live on. I did A-ball again in 1991. But in 1992 I was promoted to the Double-A Southern League.

Is minor-league umpiring a full-time job?
Not as far as making a living. But it is as far as dedication and involvement go. In the off-season, I work for UPS and a sporting goods store.

Are you nervous on the field?
I like it when fans get into the game. If a close play affects the home team, the crowd might start screaming, "Kill the umpire!" That just gets my blood going. It's motivation. I don't get nervous anymore; I get fired up.

What do you like most about the job?
I'm a part of what I love to do best—I'm a part of baseball.

What do you like least?
The travel. When you're going on a 1,200-mile road trip, you have to leave right after the game, driving through the night. By the end of a season, you're drained mentally and physically.

What advice do you have for hopefuls?
Get down and study the rule book and give it a shot. The best candidate for umpire school is someone who has never umpired before, because they have no bad habits.

Don Adam, 28,
hockey referee, American Hockey League
and International Hockey League,
Denver, Colorado.
Years in the field: six

What's your hockey background?
I started playing at age five after I saw my first game at the
University of Denver. My two older brothers and I got to
meet the players. We wanted to be like them, so our parents
let us enroll in a local [club] program.

By age 18 I was in the the United States Hockey League
(USHL) at the Junior-A level [a developmental league],
but I was cut. Then I stopped playing and concentrated on
officiating.

When did you start officiating?
When I was 12. I did games with five to seven-year-old
kids. The coaches were pretty competitive and didn't always like what we young officials did, but the kids didn't
know the difference.

How did you move up to full-time pro?
I went to three USA Hockey camps. The first was Regional
Camp, which is very competitive. We had 27 guys selected
from the western United States and 27 from the East.
You're introduced to upper-level officiating by former and
current professional officials. After that I started officiating
college hockey.

I went to National Camp the following year, where I first
met the National Hockey League officials director. I
worked in the IHL and did a second year in college hockey.
But then an IHL referee went to the USHL as referee chief
and hired me full time. After my second season in the
USHL, I got hired by the NHL at age 25.

What's your current job?
I'm in my third season as an NHL trainee. I'm not under
contract, but I am employed, supervised, scheduled and
paid by the league. I do the top minor leagues. The next
step is signing an NHL contract.

What happens when you sign an NHL contract?

They work you in slowly. You do two or three NHL exhibition games but referee the rest in the minors. In the second year, you might work up to ten games in the NHL. Over a period of three to five years, they work you up to 40 games in the NHL and 40 in the minors. After that they make a decision on whether to hire you full time into the NHL.

Is that the normal routine?

When the NHL is interested you can move up fast. I've taken some very big steps already. Promotions are based on how well you do, how many refs retire, and expansion.

You also pay your dues. The job isn't popular in the sports world because of the pressure. You give up a lot to achieve. I worked part-time jobs. I had to relocate. And you must always devote time to officiating and learning, like watching the better veteran refs to see what they do.

What do you like most?

I'm involved in my favorite sport, and I enjoy the travel. We go coast to coast. I've also been overseas, to Denmark, Finland, France, Australia and Hungary.

What do you like least?

It really bugs me that people often lack knowledge about this game. They don't know if you're doing a good job or a bad one. Hockey doesn't have much exposure yet, but we're trying to get people interested.

What are you proudest of?

I did the world championships in Finland, and I was the American referee at the [1992] Winter Olympics in France.

What's your advice for aspiring refs?

Be a student of the game. Understand the different personalities of the players and how they act in difficult situations; that helps you react and manage the game. Knowledge gives you confidence, which you will need.

Nena Roberts, 28,
basketball referee,
Apache, Oklahoma
Years in the field: seven

What's your background in sports?
I played softball, volleyball, track and basketball in high
school, but I guess basketball is in my blood. My father
played college ball.

When did you first start officiating?
In 1984 I was asked to do a grade school game. I didn't
think it would be that hard, but it was nerve-racking. I felt
really insecure. I had trouble remembering all the hand
signals. Afterward I thought I'd never do it again. But I
did, and each time it got a little bit easier.

When did you first do a high school game?
A couple of years ago. The chairman of our referees' association called and asked if I could do a junior varsity game.
I said I didn't know, but he insisted that I could. I did really
well and was pretty pleased with myself.

Do you do men's basketball?
Yes, and I like it more than women's. It's more aggressive,
and there's more action. But when we first walk onto the
court, I've noticed the guys whispering. They think someone else should come in and do the game, as if these
"girls" can't.

How do you establish control?
When you make a call, you make sure you say it like you
mean it and act like you know what you're doing. We have
an independent tournament here every year in which we
officiate grown men. I've got these huge guys, and they
come down the court arguing calls. You have to stick to
your guns.

Does that go on through the whole game?
They can get mouthy. But that doesn't bother me at all. I'm
used to it. They're just trying to play with me. Afterward
they'll come up and say, "Good game, ref." It's like a
little joke.

Does it ever get rough?
We've had a lot of fights and had to throw guys out of the gym.

What level of games do you officiate most often?
I still do more elementary than anything else. But that's the hardest to call because the kids are just learning the basics. They're walking every other dribble, and they're double dribbling. You just don't call a lot of things. These are fourth and fifth graders, and they like to ham it up. We had a tournament recently, and I got so tickled I could hardly contain myself. They all think they're Michael Jordan.

Do the parents accept your calls?
They're twice as bad as the parents of high schoolers. If they think you're picking on their kid, they'll shout at you. I've wanted to say, "Hey, shut up! Can't you see the example you're setting for your kid?" When the parents get rowdy, the kids immediately pick up on it.

How much do you get paid?
About $15 for an elementary game and $22 for a high school game. I did six games in a row one night and made $230 for the week. I suppose I could ref full time. But I own a day care center, and that's my main source of income.

What do you like best about refereeing?
A lot of women I know can't understand how or why I do it. I've had coaches in my face lots of times, and I've had to tell them to shut up and sit down. But when the horn blows, it's over. I'm proud of what I do; it's not that common for a woman to referee.

What do you like least about it?
In the small communities around here, people in the stands sometimes ask why men aren't officiating. That makes me mad, but it's funny too.

What's your advice for aspiring refs?
The most important thing is that you can't be shy. When you're on the floor, everybody else is above you in the stands, and people often watch you more than they do the players. When the whistle blows, all eyes go to the official. You have to be really confident.

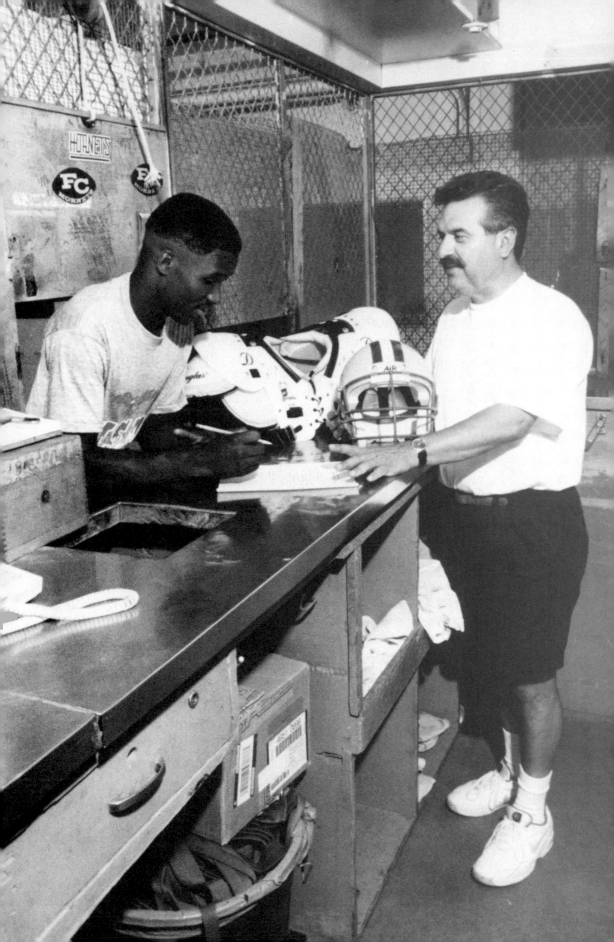

Without equipment managers the game does not go on. The first pitch of spring might never be thrown. The puck wouldn't be put in play, let alone iced. A poorly fitted football helmet might result in serious injury. When the players take center stage, the fans are entertained, and no one even notices the equipment managers—that's a sign of a job well done.

E quipment managers love sports, know sports and make sports happen, even though they don't participate in the game itself. They work for individual teams or schools where they handle several sports. They maintain every piece of equipment a team uses: its footballs, baseballs and basketballs; its uniforms, shoes and pads. They make sure that everything is organized and in its place before a game and that during a game there is a place for everything on the sideline or on the arena bench.

They also share in the glory, thrill and big bucks of modern sports. They work and live with the Michael Jordans and Barry Bonds of the world or the local college or high school hero and heroine. Winning championships translates into more glory and money for everyone, including the equipment manager.

But an equipment manager must also be willing to sweat, and not just on the field or in the weight room like the athletes and coaches. Before and after the game, he or she is at the stadium doing less-than-glamorous tasks. As an equipment manager, you'll do more laundry in a week than your mother ever made you do in a year. And you'll have to shine your shoes and the team's, too.

Plenty of jobs are out there: You only have to look to your local high school, college or professional sports team. But competition is keen. You may have to work part time or as an unpaid assistant to gain experience. Once you land a job, the pay can be low, the hours long and the opportunity for advancement limited by geography and low turnover.

Moving to the next rung on the ladder might mean moving yourself from sunny Florida to wintry Minnesota because all the jobs are filled where you live or there just aren't enough professional or school teams in your area.

Gaining experience can also be difficult. Just because you know the difference between a driver and a putter doesn't mean you can regrip a club. On-the-job training is the best route to acquiring such skills and eventually getting the job you covet. But the old catch-22 also applies: You can't get hired without experience, and you often can't get experience until you are hired. So people volunteer and work part time or broaden their skills by fixing hockey sticks for the neighborhood kids or organizing the equipment and uniforms for the local Little League club.

With new teams being created in hockey, baseball and football in the 1990s and more federally mandated money now being spent on women's sports in colleges, the demand for quality equipment managers can only increase. If you're good with your hands and determined to land a job in sports, go for it.

What You Need to Know

- ❏ Equipment used in various sports
- ❏ Rules of each sport (such as when you can come on the field if you have to or how many clubs a golfer is allowed in a bag)
- ❏ Some computer know-how (increasingly, schools and professional teams are using computers to inventory their equipment)
- ❏ Basic math (you might have to do budgets)

Necessary Skills

- ❏ Ability to fix and repair equipment
- ❏ Creative mechanical skills (dealing with unexpected damage to equipment or total breakage when you don't have replacement parts or the means to get them immediately)
- ❏ Organizational skills (team sports involve equipment for 20 to 50 players)
- ❏ A knack for keeping track of details (you may be handling and transporting equipment for several sports at once)
- ❏ Ability to drive a large truck (to transport the team's gear to away games)

Do You Have What It Takes?

- ❏ Ability to work under stress (you may have to fix equipment or find substitutes quickly)
- ❏ A thick skin (players, coaches and administrators may take their frustrations out on you)
- ❏ Patience and an easygoing nature (you'll be dealing with a wide range of personalities and, usually, some very inflated egos)
- ❏ Punctuality
- ❏ Discipline (you need to show the same level of commitment and loyalty as the athletes)

Physical Requirements

- ❏ Good personal hygiene and a neat appearance
- ❏ Reasonably good health and stamina (the job can be demanding and the hours long)
- ❏ Physical strength (you might have to load and unload equipment)

Education

A high school diploma is almost always necessary. Increasingly, equipment managers are gaining experience by assisting college teams while going to community colleges or four-year universities, although no degree for their profession exists. Employers consider any degree evidence of a disciplined and organized mind. A military background may also be helpful.

The bottom line: This is still a job that relies more on experience, aptitude and mechanical ability than on any degree or certificate.

Licenses Required

None. But if you're responsible for transporting the equipment to away games, you may need a special license for driving a large truck.

Job Outlook

Job opportunities: growing but competitive

Job opportunities exist at most high schools, colleges and even amateur sports clubs. Once dominated by former janitors and field maintenance workers, the role of equipment manager is now more professionally attractive and thus more competitive.

At the professional sports level, jobs are scarcer and more difficult to obtain. Years of apprenticeship are necessary. The best opportunities are in expanding sports, such as hockey and baseball.

Entry-level job: assistant or student equipment manager

You'll gain valuable experience, but the job will mainly consist of the dirty work the senior equipment manager doesn't have to do anymore.

Beginners

- ❑ Clean up locker rooms (pick up wet and dirty uniforms and towels; mop the showers)
- ❑ Set out pregame food (for the athletes and coaches)
- ❑ Clean, polish and repair equipment
- ❑ Set up the playing field (anything from painting the lines to erecting a soccer net)
- ❑ Tote the equipment onto and off the field
- ❑ Distribute towels to players
- ❑ Take inventory of the equipment
- ❑ Load and unload equipment from the van, truck or plane for away games
- ❑ Launder, fold and store uniforms

Supervisors or senior equipment managers

May include any of the above, plus:
- ❑ Hire and train assistants
- ❑ Order new equipment and parts
- ❑ Prepare equipment budgets
- ❑ Consult with coaches, administrators and owners
- ❑ Keep the players happy (including making arrangements for picking up relatives and friends at airports)

During the season, which can last from three months (high school football) to nine (professional sports), the average week is six days of well over 40 hours. Night games usually mean working until midnight. Most managers also start early in the morning, game or no game, just to keep on top of things.

High school and college sports are often played both

during the week and on weekends. Professional sports always involve weekend work and holidays.

The hours are often less demanding for equipment managers at small high schools, community colleges, or even universities, where the job may not involve that many sports or the school may hire people to work shifts. If a school doesn't have athletic teams, the equipment manager handles only the equipment needed for classes or intramural sports. Or, as is the case with some state universities, the job is considered a civil service position and can be almost a nine-to-five arrangement.

Time Off ◆ High school and college equipment managers have some summer months off, although football practice usually starts in August. You might need a summer job to supplement your income. Small-school managers often have an easier pace and scheduled vacation time.

Traditional periods off during Easter and Christmas might be spent working if the school's team goes on to a state championship tournament, a bowl game or even a foreign tour. Some equipment managers also spend vacation time doing extra duties, such as budgets and inventory.

Professional sports have almost no off-season anymore, with clinics, training camps, scouting combines (where potential players for an upcoming draft are tested and evaluated) and exhibition schedules. Equipment managing is a job for people who live to work, not those who work to live. Vacation time may total two to three weeks annually.

Perks ◆ ❏ Opportunities to share in team victories
❏ Bonuses for championships at the professional level
❏ Travel to away games with expenses paid
❏ Local recognition
❏ Free tickets (sometimes) for friends and family

❑ High schools
❑ Community colleges
❑ Four-year colleges and universities
❑ Professional sports teams, at both the major- and
   minor-league levels

◆ **Who's Hiring**

Beginners and experienced equipment managers:
local travel for some; frequent cross-country travel for those
who work for teams

◆ **Places You'll Go**

High school equipment managers generally travel only
locally. But if the school is in a sparsely populated area,
they may travel farther—up to several hundred miles is not
that unusual—just to play their regular schedule.

Equipment managers who work at the big colleges and
in the pros often visit major metropolitan areas where playing facilities are located, crisscrossing the country several
times during a season. College teams often make trips to
rural college towns to play competitors.

Foreign tours are also becoming popular as some high
schools and colleges and many pro teams are actively trying
to export their games. That means visits to places ranging
from England to Russia to Japan and sometimes Australia
and Scandinavia.

Equipment managers work in locker rooms, stadiums
and arenas and on the field. It can be extremely cold or hot
both inside and out, depending on the facility. It's also
noisy, sometimes chaotic, and full of less-than-fragrant
smells. After a game, locker room work often means slop-
ping around in rivers of dirty water as the shower stalls
overflow.

◆ **Surroundings**

On the sidelines of a stadium, the noise level can ap-
proach ear-shattering proportions from school bands, piped-
in rock music, exploding scoreboards and, of course, fans.
Inside an arena, the noise is even worse and the work area
is often cramped, hot and sticky.

Dollars and Cents

High school equipment managers make $12,000 to $20,000 a year. You can, however, often work overtime for extra bucks, doing anything from acting as a hall monitor to lining fields and setting up tracks.

Colleges and universities pay $15,000 to $40,000, depending on their size and the range of responsibilities.

Professional teams pay from $45,000 to $70,000, plus a possible bonus for play-offs and championships that can boost some salaries to around $90,000.

Moving Up

The logical place to start is at a high school or college. Few equipment managers start with professional teams, but some opportunities exist in growing sports such as hockey and baseball.

An equipment manager builds his or her reputation through the word-of-mouth network within the profession. You'll succeed by performing your job in such a smooth, professional way that athletes and coaches can get on with their jobs with a minimum of hassle.

Where the Jobs Are

Where the sports teams are, which is just about anywhere. The better-paying jobs with professional teams are generally found in the bigger cities, although some major colleges are located in small towns.

Training

No formal training or degree exists, although some colleges are now offering courses in managing and repairing equipment. The best training is on-the-job experience.

The Male/Female Equation

Only five to ten percent of all equipment managers are women. That's changing rapidly, however, especially since Congress passed Title IX legislation mandating that women's college sports be put on more equal footing with men's. It's difficult for women to gain experience unless they know the sport. And most sports are still played by men. Employers can, and do, cite that as a consideration for not hiring.

The Bad News

❑ Low pay, especially for beginners
❑ Hard work and long hours, including weekends and holidays
❑ Athletes, coaches and administrators can be demanding and difficult
❑ Moving up can be slow and may require relocation

The Good News

❑ Good money awaits the highly successful
❑ You're an insider
❑ You'll be around athletes and a game you love
❑ You can tell your grandchildren you knew the next Joe Montana

◆ **Making Your Decision: What to Consider**

Athletic Equipment Managers Association
723 Keil Court
Bowling Green, Ohio 43402
419-352-1207

AEMA holds an annual convention for members to network, attend clinics and brush up on the latest trends.

◆ **More Information Please**

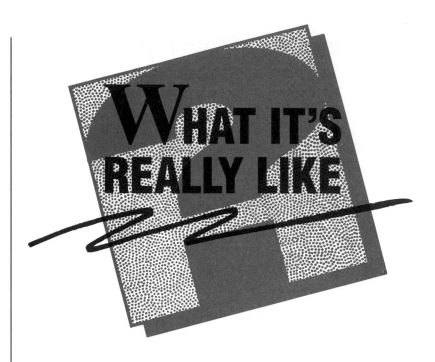

WHAT IT'S REALLY LIKE

Jim Conant, 42,
equipment manager,
Westwood High School,
Mesa, Arizona
Years in the field: five

How did you break into this field?
I've always loved sports, but I worked in construction for
18 years because I had a wife and kids to feed. When the
company tried to go nonunion and asked me to take a pay
cut, I wrote a letter of resignation.

I put my application in at several places in the school dis-
trict. The equipment manager of a high school got sick, so
the school asked if I would be interested in a temporary
job. And I remembered what my dad had said once: If you
get a chance to do something you want, even if it's temporary, go out and do it, because it might work into something
more permanent.

I worked really hard; the place was a mess and disorgan-
ized. I made myself available to the coaches. I also worked
some weekends to get the place shipshape because I really
wanted the job.

Why did you want the job so much?

I'm such a big sports fan, and this seemed tailor-made for me. It's like something that came from heaven. Now I look forward to going to work every day.

How did you convince the school you had the qualifications for this job?

I told them I had great energy and was a dedicated individual. I said I was looking for a challenge and thought I was capable of doing anything I put my mind to. For eight years I had volunteered to talk to prison inmates about personal growth and self-confidence. The school liked that. They figured if I could deal with inmates, I could deal with the kids.

How long did it take for the temporary job to become permanent?

Only about two months. The football team went on to the play-offs, then won the state championship. So I was in the right place at the right time. The next day the principal asked me if I would consider staying here, and I said yes.

What kind of preparation did you have for being an equipment manager?

I played sports in high school. But a lot of this job is hands-on learning. The day I was hired, I called another equipment manager and went to look at his room. I tried to apply what I saw.

What's the most important thing you had to learn?

How to fit the [football] helmets properly. If they aren't fitted right, the kids are going to get hurt. I joined the [equipment managers] association to learn more and went to their clinic at USC [the University of Southern California]. It's crucial to continue educating yourself.

Describe your job responsibilities.

I'm in charge of maintaining the equipment, keeping the stock up-to-date, ordering new stock and making sure we get our stuff back. I'm also one of the few managers who does a budget. I do about half of it, and the coaches do the other half. Then we allocate the money to each sport. I also do the laundry—between 40 and 56 uniforms after a game.

How long is your week?
About 55 to 60 hours during the football season and 45
hours a week in the spring. I work five days a week and an
extra three hours or so on the weekend.

At budget time I have to come in at 6 A.M. After games I'm
here until midnight, then back in on Saturdays for a few
hours. We almost went all the way to the state championships in football this year, so that means ten weeks of regular season, then three play-off games. You're looking at 13
weeks of Fridays away from home. That's a lot of hours.

This is a young man's job. I'm not saying an older man
can't do it, but it takes a lot of energy to keep coaches and
administrators off your back and to stay on top of things.

What do you like most about your work?
The challenge of getting everything to run very smoothly. I
like having things organized. But I also like my job because
it changes all the time, from fall to winter to spring sports.
I take some satisfaction in knowing I'm doing the job right,
so a kid doesn't get hurt.

What do you like least about your work?
Trying to get equipment returned. Things can disappear
real quick. Sometimes I have to chase people down.

What has your proudest achievement been?
Overcoming the mess we had here several years ago. Every
room was like a dungeon. I was able to straighten this place
up and make it functional while sports were going on. It's
nice now when people come in and say I have a neat equipment room.

Being part of a state championship team my first year was
also a highlight. I've been part of five state championships
in different sports now, and the appreciation of the coaches
is great.

**What advice would you give to someone who's thinking
about going into this field?**
If I could catch that person as a sophomore in high school,
I would tell him or her to start getting some experience
then. I have three student managers who have been helping
me here for three years. They will get a half credit for their

work and will be able to apply for a job and say they have experience. Plus I'll give them a reference.

Kathy Majoras, 30,
equipment manager,
Lorain County Community College,
Elyria, Ohio
Years in the field: ten

How did you start your career?
When I was 19 years old I had a chance to work full time, make money and get benefits. When the equipment manager here retired, I applied for the job—I had been working for her as the assistant equipment manager—and when I got my two-year degree in general studies, I got the job.

What do you like about your job?
I love sports. It's not a job where you come in every day and do the exact same thing. You're not confined to sitting behind a desk. Every day is a different challenge. It also allows me to do after-hours coaching.

Did coaching help prepare you for this job?
Yes. I had coached high school volleyball, basketball and softball as an assistant.

What else helped prepare you for it?
I grew up in a family with four brothers. We played football, basketball, hockey, baseball—you name it, we played it. And I pretty much held my own, except when I tried to jump rope with the girls and broke my foot.

What do you currently do?
I order the equipment for our physical education classes and recreational activities. I also oversee my student staff in the equipment room area, usually eight to ten students per quarter. I schedule the use of our indoor and outdoor tennis courts, cross-country course, gymnasium, field house and track by outside renters. I write a weekly department newsletter and articles for the college newspaper. I order and handle the distribution of recreation and intramural awards, including designing tee shirts for the awards.

What do you like most about your work?

Interacting with the people I meet, the students and the people from the community—teenagers to people in their seventies—who come to our fitness center. I also like being finished with my job by two o'clock in the afternoon.

What's the worst thing about the job?

Having to start work at six in the morning, which means getting up at 4:30 A.M. And sometimes people come in to use the facilities and don't know the rules. Some want to argue with you.

What have you done that you are most proud of?

We started a Toys for Tots volleyball tournament here that is three years old now. I came up with the idea. To participate you have to bring a new toy, which is donated to a disadvantaged child. It's a very successful event, and it's nice to be able to give something back to the community.

What advice would you give someone interested in this field?

Having a background in athletics is very helpful, of course. You have to play the sports and know the equipment. Someone who wants to do this job should also be well organized and have a lot of patience.

Ed Wagner Jr., 36,
equipment manager, New York Giants, East Rutherford, New Jersey
Years in the field: 16

How did you get your start with the Giants?

I was an assistant here for two years. I started working in the visitor's locker room on game days. Then the equipment manager took a liking to me and brought me into the Giants locker room on Sundays, and then eventually during the week for practices.

What kind of preparation did you have?

I didn't play sports in high school. But I loved football and had season tickets to Giants games. I worked as a carpenter when I first came out of school.

Describe what you do now.

We are responsible for the ordering, distribution, fitting, maintenance and general upkeep of the equipment during the season. We also open up and close the buildings.

How important is it to know about proper fitting of equipment?

The fitting of helmets is crucial. A guy's career depends on how well you can do that.

How about the ordering and distribution end?

We handle a pretty big budget here—in the hundreds of thousands of dollars. You have to know merchandise and materials. And you have to recognize quality. You have to keep up with the trends in the industry in textiles and plastic and padding and foam—things you will be using every day.

Despite the detail stuff, most people would think this is a pretty glamorous job. Is it?

There is glamour for the three and a half hours when you play on Sunday afternoons or Monday nights. It's also glamorous when you win, but not so much when you lose. My job really relies on whether or not something is going to break down, when a problem might get a guy out of the game for a play. That could be crucial, so you try to make sure nothing happens.

How do you do that?

You prepare things in advance. If you are going away for a cold-weather game, you make sure you have the proper equipment so the players can go out there and not worry about being cold. You make them comfortable, and that helps them do their job.

Is it pretty intense for you during a game?

I don't wander the sidelines watching the game. I see very little of it. I have one spot where I stand, so the players know exactly where I am if anything goes wrong. I've seen guys who broke their belts and played by holding their pants up with one hand. If there is a problem, I'm ready.

What's it like to work with the players?

You are dealing with 50 different personalities every day, and they aren't the usual kind of guys who you might work next to on a regular job. These are high-profile people, and some do have attitudes. I spend more time with them than I do with my family during the season.

What are your hours like?
We work seven days a week during the season—we average 12 to 15 hours a day for four out of the seven. Otherwise we work practices—doing laundry, fixing the equipment.

What's the best part of the job?
Just being associated with a professional team like this one. Even though you're not a player, you do feel like you're part of this game. And I like knowing that there are only 28 of us in the world [one for each NFL team] who can do what we are doing right now. You also rub elbows with quality people in this game. And going to the Super Bowl is a great feeling.

Do you get a Super Bowl share?
Yes, we do. And we are awarded a ring. Plus my wife and daughter got presents from the Giants.

What's the worst part of the job?
The first few weeks of training camp are tough. A lot of players are fighting for a job, and that means a lot of pressure. And with two practices a day and hot weather, you have a lot of work. You are also dealing with double the squad, up to 80 guys, as opposed to 40-some during the season. It makes for 16-hour days.

What are you proudest of after 16 years?
Probably going to two Super Bowls. Also, there are players who go from here to other teams and tell people what high regard they hold you in. It makes you feel proud and an integral part of the team.

What advice would you give people who want to do this?
This is a being-in-the-right-place-at-the-right-time sort of job. You have to get into a good sports program at a good school and then get your name known as someone who does a good job. Be trustworthy and willing to start at the bottom.

Once you're in, what does it take to be successful?
You really have to love the job and make a total commitment to it. You must be willing to give up time with your family—almost six or seven months each year if you work for a professional team. And whether the team wins or loses, you have to keep doing your job. You can never let yourself lay back and take it easy.

Lights, camera, action! Sure, that's a movie cliché. But it also describes what the sports photographer or videographer does. You have fun capturing the action, then enjoy seeing your work replayed on television or splashed across the morning paper or magazine covers. Achieve more success and your work is trumpeted by video clubs or graces the pages of those slick, large-format books featuring sports heroes and heroines.

magine experiencing the Super Bowl live or having a courtside seat for the royal pomp of Wimbledon or a dugout view of the World Series. You call this work? You bet it is. "Grin and grippers," as veteran photographers call hopeful amateurs, need not apply.

Sports photography calls for a brilliant eye for framing

action and making it fresh each time. It's a highly developed skill, acquired by putting in hundreds of hours. You must be a natural artist and an experienced technician.

The competition is fierce, and photo editors expect you to get the picture they saw watching the game from their living room couch. The football field may be 100 yards long and the baseball diamond 420 feet to deep center, but position is everything, and you've got to be in the right place at the right time, even if it means clawing your way through dozens of people.

Getting a great shot may also mean hours on the sidelines in sub-zero weather or behind the basket in a sweaty arena. Hazards abound. Athletes tumble off playing areas, and it's often the sports photographer who gets creamed by someone twice his or her size. The camera may end up lodged in an eye socket or a rib cage.

Sports photographers work for newspapers, magazines and wire services. They can also land staff jobs at public relations firms, advertising agencies and video production companies. Freelance work is often on a per-shot basis, but sometimes it's for lengthy projects.

A growing number of photographers also earn bucks through stock agencies—photo libraries that store your work. When editors call looking for pictures of a pole vaulter or a swimmer, or a nice composition of mountains and skiers, the agency sells the shot and pays you a fee. The catch? Struggling freelancers must spend money up front, shooting pictures someone *might* want someday. But when you are finally established, it's all gravy.

Many still photographers are now switching to video, where the market is growing. Sports videographers, who may be freelancers or part of a team, tape practices, training camps, exhibition games and regular-season matches.

Videographers break down the tape for coaches, competing teams, the league office and owners. It's a pressure-cooker job because coaches live by tape. Botch the assignment, miss one crucial tackle and you're shown the door.

If you've got a knack for taking good shots on film or tape, shoot as much as you can, even if it's just a Little League game or a high school swimming meet. A great picture is a great picture, and it could be enough to impress a photo editor.

What You Need to Know

◆ **Getting into the Field**

- ❏ The ins and outs of the sports you're covering
- ❏ Lenses, films and equipment: what to use when
- ❏ Principles of composition and perspective
- ❏ Properties of light (especially for black-and-white photography)
- ❏ The color spectrum (and how it registers on film)
- ❏ Photographic history and trends (for inspiration and to keep ahead of the competition)
- ❏ Techniques of film developing and printing or tape editing
- ❏ Computers (for graphics and video work)

Necessary Skills

- ❏ Ability to photograph or videotape fast-moving action
- ❏ Ability to edit videotape or print photographs
- ❏ Ability to light difficult areas
- ❏ Ability to fix equipment or improvise on location
- ❏ Good communication (especially the ability to put people at ease for portrait work)

Do You Have What It Takes?

- ❏ Deep interest in the sports you shoot
- ❏ An eye for pictures
- ❏ Ability to work under deadlines
- ❏ Creative flair
- ❏ Ability to anticipate a picture
- ❏ Understanding of where to position yourself
- ❏ Patience (you may have to shoot rolls or hours of film or tape to get what you want, or wait hours or days for the right shot)
- ❏ Thick skin (to deal with rejection from those judging your photos and the rudeness of some athletes and coaches)
- ❏ Business sense (freelancers spend more time marketing than shooting)

Physical Requirements

- ❏ Strength to lift and hold photographic equipment for long periods
- ❏ Manual dexterity (to easily change lenses and load film or tape and to manipulate equipment efficiently)

Education

No formal education is required, but experience counts for a lot. Some employers want photographers with a college degree, but few will turn away one with an excellent portfolio.

Licenses Required

None, although most photographers need press credentials to work sporting events. If you're not affiliated with a newspaper or magazine, join an organization like the American Society of Media Photographers, the Advertising Photographers of America or the National Press Photographers Association. You'll get an identification card that might help establish your professionalism.

Job Outlook ◆ **Competition for jobs:** very competitive
With the number of newspapers and magazines shrinking, fewer staff jobs and freelance assignments are available. Video is offering new opportunities.

The Ground Floor ◆ **Entry-level job:** photographer or videographer's assistant; newspaper stringer
You can gain valuable experience and knowledge of how to use equipment as an assistant, but you will be limited to the sports or areas the photographer you assist covers. Stringers often start out by shooting anything and everything the newspaper asks them to, from car crashes to the occasional Little League game. Videographers often start by shooting elementary and high school sports.

Beginners

- ❏ Change lenses and film for photographer or video-grapher
- ❏ Develop and print film or edit videotape
- ❏ Set up lights and backgrounds
- ❏ Make sure clients have a chair or anything else they want
- ❏ Pack and transport equipment
- ❏ Answer the phone and take care of paperwork—and fetch coffee

Experienced photographers/videographers

- ❏ Hire and train assistants (if you're lucky enough to afford them)
- ❏ Supervise studio and/or darkroom employees
- ❏ Develop ad or PR campaigns for sports manufacturers and teams or photo essays for magazines
- ❏ Shoot sports events, personalities and merchandise
- ❏ Teach photography part time at workshops, schools and seminars
- ❏ Develop new clients and business (freelancers)

◆ **On-the-Job Responsi-bilities**

Sports photographers with newspapers and magazines often work a fairly standard five-day week, although that might include late nights or weekends. Expect to put in long hours, especially when covering big sporting events. Videographers who are employed by teams travel with them and work irregular hours.

Freelancers work anytime they can. When on assignment, most work straight through to completion, which could mean a 12-hour day or a six-month stint.

◆ **When You'll Work**

Many staff photographers are regularly scheduled to work on weekends when games are played. Those who work full time for newspapers and magazines get the same amount of vacation time as other employees.

◆ **Time Off**

Freelancers can take time off when work is slow or during the off-season, but they are often too jittery about where the next check is coming from to plan ahead. That means sometimes taking off at a moment's notice.

Perks

❏ Access to athletes and sports figures
❏ Expense accounts when on assignment
❏ Free film and darkroom supplies, or deep discounts (especially when doing advertising work)
❏ Sports merchandise discounts (again, when doing advertising work)

Who's Hiring

❏ Newspapers, wire services and magazines
❏ Sports teams, especially professional teams
❏ Advertising and public relations firms
❏ Video production companies

On-the-Job Hazards

❏ Possibility of injury if the action gets too close to you
❏ Aches and pains from hauling heavy equipment around

Places You'll Go

Beginners and experienced photographers: little to extensive travel
You might just cover the sports teams in your area, but most successful photographers travel extensively around the country or even abroad.

Surroundings

You may work at stadiums, arenas, pools or rinks, on golf courses or courts, or on mountainsides. Those who do advertising or corporate and public relations work often shoot in studios or other inside locations. Once shooting or taping is finished, you may complete the work in a darkroom or editing facilities, which can be cramped, stuffy and hot and smell of chemicals.

Full-time staff photographers make $7,000 to $20,000 at small-circulation papers. Bigger papers pay from $15,000 to $60,000+. Magazine staff photographers make from $10,000 to $100,000. **◆Dollars and Cents**

Freelancers earn $5 to $75 for a picture published in a newspaper. A Sunday supplement cover might earn $100 to $250. A magazine cover can command anywhere from $200 to $2,000; a photo essay might bring $3,000. Often there is a day rate: The best freelancers get $600 to $800 a day plus expenses.

Ad agencies, PR firms and video production companies pay better freelance rates than newspapers and magazines. Ad agencies in New York and California pay $1,000 to $2,000 a day. In other places the average is more like $150 to $600. A videographer might make $5 to $15 a hour, or $50 to $300 a day, in a midwestern state, but twice that on the coasts. Top photographers can command $6,000 to $10,000 a day.

Photographers often spend at least five to ten years on a staff job before going freelance. They then live off savings for a year or more while they set up a studio, compile a stock library and/or portfolio and develop a list of clients. Freelancers often find success by specializing in a particular sport. **◆Moving Up**

Those who stay with the same publication usually go from shooting small sports events to major pro sports. The more experienced a photographer is and the more prestigious the sports, the more money earned. Another path up is to move to a bigger paper or magazine or go into PR and ad agency work.

Videographers follow similar paths, although some also film weddings and business conventions. Top videographers may take a job on a professional sports team or work in-house for a production company hired by sports franchises, manufacturers or promoters.

Where the Jobs Are

There are more opportunities in major metropolitan areas where the media and sports teams are concentrated. Heading the list is the New York metropolitan area; close behind are Chicago, Los Angeles, San Francisco, Boston, Atlanta, Detroit, St. Louis, Miami, Houston, Dallas, Phoenix, Seattle, Salt Lake City, Cleveland and Portland.

Training

Classroom instruction and access to darkroom facilities are a must for would-be sports photographers. Some vocational/technical high schools and many community colleges offer both. The book *Photographer's Market* lists seminars and workshops in the back of its annual edition. Photography clubs are another way to improve your techniques and build contacts.

The Male/Female Equation

An estimated five percent of all sports photographers are women, many of whom work part time. With an increase in women's sports teams at high schools and colleges, more women are now shooting games, matches and events. Many women have earned a name for themselves by seizing on a specialty the men tend to ignore—equestrian events, gymnastics, rodeos or women's sports.

Making Your Decision: What to Consider

The Bad News

❑ Stiff competition
❑ Physically demanding work
❑ Exposure to harsh weather conditions
❑ Deadline pressure
❑ Low pay for beginners and some freelancers

The Good News

❑ Creative satisfaction
❑ Excitement of being close to the action
❑ Chance to be a part of sports you love
❑ Good money if you're successful
❑ Opportunity to work with top sports figures

American Society of Media Photographers
419 Park Avenue South
New York, New York 10016
212-889-9144

ASMP members receive a monthly magazine about industry trends and have their names listed in an annual directory, which helps establish a working roster for editors and other employers seeking qualified photographers.

National Press Photographers Association
3200 Croasdaile Drive, Suite 306
Durham, North Carolina 27705
919-383-7246

NPPA sponsors numerous workshops and seminars throughout the country.

◆ **More Information Please**

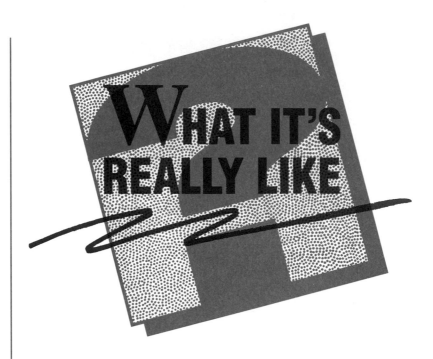

WHAT IT'S REALLY LIKE

Walter Iooss, Jr., 49,
freelance sports photographer,
New York, New York
Years in the business: 31

How did you get started in sports photography?
My father was a hobbyist and bought a 300 millimeter
lens—a telephoto—as his first lens. We'd sit in the stands
and shoot pictures of high school football games. When I
was 16, I called up *Sports Illustrated.* Even though I was
just a kid, the assistant picture editor agreed to look at my
pictures. He told me to stay in touch and got me credentials
once in a while to go to games.

When did you sell your first picture?
In high school I sold *Sports Illustrated* a black-and-white
photo from a Princeton-Columbia University football
game. Things just kept rolling from there. I even organized
football and basketball games with my friends and shot
pictures of them. People get too hung up on the idea that
you have to do a big game or that you need a lot of fancy
equipment.

How long did it take you to become established?
I was a contributing photographer for *Sports Illustrated* by the time I was 19. I shot football games, pro and occasionally college, on a freelance basis. Football was the thing I could really do well.

I was living at home. My father decided to give me two years to start making it. And then if nothing happened I was supposed to go to college and try again when I came back out. That almost happened, but another photographer canceled an assignment, so they sent me to Buffalo for an American Football League game. This was 1962, and Jack Kemp was the quarterback and Elbert "Golden Wheels" Dubenion ran a 103-yard kick off back for a touchdown. I had the whole sequence. From that point on, I was working every week.

Have you ever shot a swimsuit issue?
I shot Kathy Ireland for the 1993 issue, and I've done a couple of other issues in the past. But sports is what I do best.

What other sports have you done?
I've shot baseball, basketball, golf and tennis. I did the Super Bowl this year, but that's the only football game I do anymore.

What's the best thing about your job?
The best thing is simple. I love to take pictures of athletes, and I'm getting paid to do what I want to do.

The worst thing?
Travel sometimes gets to be too much. I don't have the energy level I used to have. I'm in really good shape, and I still have all the enthusiasm I ever did when I'm working. But I've been doing it for 31 years, and I can feel some of the air being slowly let out of the balloon.

What's your proudest achievement?
I'd say one of them was an Olympic project with Fuji [film], starting in 1982, when Fuji was basically an unknown commodity in the United States. They hired me for two and a half years to try to generate interest and get professional photographers to switch to their film.

I documented American athletes as they trained toward the 1984 games in Los Angeles. We did a book and had exhibits all over the U.S., including the Smithsonian in Washington. After a year and a half, everybody on the field at the Olympic trials was using Fuji film.

Are you still working for *Sports Illustrated*?
I still do occasional assignments for *Sports Illustrated,* but for the last five years I've been doing mostly advertising work—anything to do with sports. I did Camel cigarettes for five years. It was one of the greatest jobs I ever had because I traveled to the Philippines, Thailand, Malaysia, Bora Bora, Hawaii and Australia. The down side in advertising is that you're restricted artistically. But that's where all the money is.

How do you balance that with your desire for artistic freedom?
Right now I'm doing a book with Michael Jordan, traveling all over with him. I'm shooting the greatest athlete in the world. There's nothing I'd rather be doing.

What advice would you give aspiring photographers?
I'd recommend they go to college. Not many people are hiring kids who are 17 or 18 anymore; it's difficult to break in. If the college has a high-powered sports program, you can get great experience shooting for the college newspaper. But if you're really talented and you have a portfolio that is unique—even just out of high school—someone will look at it. The other critical thing is drive—you've got to really want to do it.

Brian Badzinski, 31,
assistant video director,
New Orleans Saints,
New Orleans, Louisiana.
Years in the field: seven

How did you get into video?
I've always been good with electronics, and I've always had a curiosity about photography. I never really got into

still photography on a professional level, but video—which is the combination of photography and electronics—caught my interest.

I started doing weddings for friends and people who had kids playing basketball in high school. I got $20 here, $50 there. Then I started getting more serious. I saw there was demand for this type of work. I tried to perfect what I was doing, to be more professional.

When did you get your job with the Saints?
I was working in cable, as a technician and installer. I was 24. I started coming around on my days off and volunteering to help with the transition from film to video. Every team needs to get film from colleges, but colleges only give it to certain people. We started combining the college films and transferring them to videotape so everyone could have more access to college games. The Saints needed a lot of this work done, so they offered me the job on a temporary basis.

I was working full-time hours but as a part-time employee, like an internship. I did that for a couple of years, and finally the head video guy retired and everybody moved up the ladder one step. Then I became assistant video person.

What do you do for the Saints?
During the week we shoot practices, edit the tapes, break them down and make copies for the coaches. We also break down tapes from opponents for evaluation and game planning. We film our games and make copies for our coaches and our opponents. And we get tape from colleges, copy it and break it down and send it out to scouts.

Can a modern coach function without tape?
It's pretty vital to an NFL football team these days. If for some reason we couldn't give our coaches tapes and the other team did, they could give the team a basic game plan, but they really wouldn't be able to put a scheme together to combat what the other guys do. I would say better than 50 percent of what they do is study the films.

What's the best thing about your job?
I contribute to the team's success. That makes people happy. It's a great feeling. On the other hand, when you're

with a losing team, it makes you sick to your stomach. But you keep doing your job and hope things turn around.

What's the worst thing about the job?
The hours and being away from my family. During training camp we'll put in over 100-hour weeks. During the season, we put in close to 80-hour weeks.

If you were starting out today, would you try to get your basic training in high school?
Yes. The more experience you get and the more you become accustomed to what you're shooting, the better you become at your art. Get involved as much as possible in shooting sports in high school or college.

And realize you're really not in the limelight. Players and coaches are in the limelight. Make sure it's what you want to do, because it's really tough and really demanding on family life. But I love it—it's probably the first job where I ever enjoyed coming in every morning, even when I'm filming a practice in the rain for hours.

Jeff Burkholder, 30, commercial and sports photographer, Life Images, Sacramento, California
Years in the business: ten

How did you get started?
My dad had a camera, and I used to swipe it every time I could. In high school I took pictures of the football and track teams. Then I signed up to be a school newspaper photographer at college, even though I didn't know much about taking and developing pictures. Before my first assignment—which was to shoot the cross-country team—I read a Kodak photography book. My photo won third place in the California community college photojournalism competition.

So being a photographer for the school newspaper was good training?

It was like taking the most advanced class possible. I was photo editor for three semesters and shot 15 to 20 rolls a week. I started sending things to the *Sacramento Bee* newspaper and the Associated Press. And I hung around every photographer I could find at sporting events to get tips from them.

Did you make any money from your photography?

Some. But once I really got hooked on photography, I did darkroom work for a magazine from 4 to 8 A.M. Then I'd go to school, and I'd work at a restaurant at night. All my money went into film and equipment.

Did you graduate from the community college?

I never got my degree. I had changed my major to journalism and photography, and then I changed colleges. But the excitement of photography and the deadlines lured me away from school.

What was your first photography job?

I started working at a 12-page weekly newspaper in my hometown. I worked 70 hours a week and made $100, but it was probably the most fun I've ever had, and it was a learning experience.

Were you selling photographs anywhere else?

I was listed as the number four stringer for the local AP bureau. Gradually I did more for the AP, and then I got a job for the *Sacramento Bee*'s weekly regional section, where about 60 percent of the work was sports.

How long did that job last?

Only about nine months—I got laid off during budget cuts. But I was doing a lot of freelance work for *Sacramento* magazine and the AP, and I picked up work as a salesman for a camera store where I'd been going for years. That job paid the rent, and I got discounts on equipment.

Eventually I started getting assignments from a local magazine for business executives. I did a lot of sports assignments, but I also got to branch out into portraits.

Sports is great and fun, but the scrambling and racing for a position can get tiresome after a while. I did get to do some interesting sports assignments shooting marathons and triathlons for *Triathlon* magazine, *Runner's World* and *Winning,* a cycling magazine.

What happened next?
About the middle of 1989, the photo editor for a small newspaper asked me to come work with him. That was great because we pushed each other to do better work. I won three awards for the paper in sports, news and features.

I left because I couldn't afford it anymore. I was covering my own insurance, using my own equipment and driving my own vehicle. I was making $4.25 an hour. They offered me a dollar-an-hour raise, but I turned it down. That was in early 1990; since then, I've been on my own.

How long has it taken you to get established?
I'm still getting established. I decided to do more corporate communications, working for company publications and doing portraits.

What are you doing currently?
I do executive portraits, corporate brochures and magazine work. The most recent sports work I did was for a magazine piece on the business of the Sacramento Kings (an NBA team). I spent three days and nights shooting at the Arco arena, photographing everything from the guys making hot dogs to the popcorn vendors up in the stands to the basketball game itself.

What do you like best about what you do?
The freedom of being my own boss. I pick and choose my assignments because I know where my work is going, and I'm not going to jeopardize my standards.

What do you like least?
The paperwork. And clients who think we just push buttons and want to pay us accordingly. They don't understand that we are creating an image and putting our names on it.

What advice would you give those starting out in photography?

Know your sport and study your craft. Photography is becoming so technical that it's hard to get the experience on your own. Junior college is a great place to learn and screw up—which you will—rather than later on, when it counts. Or get a job as an assistant, which is a great way to learn the craft and the business.

Also, figure out if you really can handle the stress of deadlines. Sometimes the work is dangerous. I broke two ribs doing a [San Francisco] 49ers game. And your back and knees will hurt later in life. Mine do, and I'm only 30 years old. But I love being a photographer.

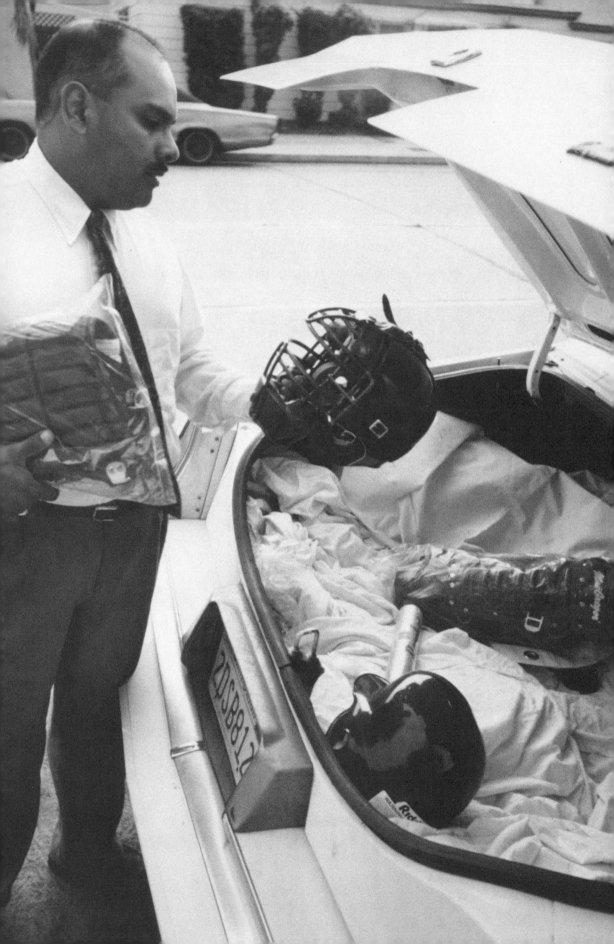

"Can you believe this new driver? It's graphite, light as a feather, and it socks the ball a mile. Your customers will love this baby." The pitch of a sporting goods representative might remind you of a conversation on the links. If you're lucky, you'll get to sell equipment, clothing or footwear connected with a sport you play or like, whether it's golf, tennis or a team sport.

Manufacturer's representatives love sports and talking about the latest hot products. They spend their days visiting sporting goods stores and teams in their territory. Sometimes they're successful in convincing a new account to take on a product or line or an established account to increase its orders. Sometimes they're not.

Reps will tell you that a "win" feels as good as kicking

73

the deciding field goal in overtime or hitting a perfect draw over water. It gets in their blood. It's exciting and challenging, and there's nothing else they'd rather do.

Only about 15 percent of the reps in the industry are on manufacturers' payrolls. The rest earn commissions—a fixed percent on each sale. The more they sell, the bigger their income. To be a successful rep, you have to be self-motivated and highly disciplined. You schedule your own appointments, devise your own sales pitch and figure out how to service the clients within your territory.

Reps understand the products they tout; some are jocks who once played on the team they're now trying to sell to. Some start in retail, where they get to know the products they might handle later on as a rep. Others learn the ropes at the pro shop of a country club, ski resort or tennis facility, where they can also make contacts among the manufacturers.

Reps who are employees of manufacturers often start in entry-level jobs in inventory or customer relations to learn about the market and the product. Beginners sometimes get less desirable lines and territories that more experienced reps have moved on from.

The independents often work out of their home or open an agency with several other reps to pool their expertise, contacts and some expenses. But like others who own their own businesses, these reps must cover most of their costs—transportation, entertainment and long-distance phone calls—out of their own pocket.

Outgoing by nature, reps are often quick-witted, articulate and personable. They are great conversationalists on the phone and in person. They are comfortable entertaining clients, taking them to sporting events or out to dinner. They develop a keen sense of who will buy and when, why they will buy and if they can be counted on to pay.

A rep has to be thick-skinned; rejection is a way of life. But a "yes," particularly if it's a major order, is all that's needed to make your day or your week—even your year.

If you love to talk sports and sports equipment, like the idea of being your own boss and have the maturity and personality to structure your own work day, becoming a sales rep for a sports manufacturer may be your niche in the world of sports.

What You Need to Know

❏ Equipment, apparel and shoes specific to a sport (certain stores cater to certain sports; teams have needs specific to their sport)
❏ Changes and innovations in sports equipment
❏ Business trends (what your competition is doing)
❏ Fashion trends (what clothes are being worn by athletes and fans)
❏ Computers (for working with inventories, sales orders and product information)

Necessary Skills

❏ Ability to place calls to strangers and engage them in conversation
❏ Ability to deliver an effective sales pitch
❏ Basic math (to compute discounts and order totals and track expenses)

Do You Have What It Takes?

❏ Ability to drive long distances without getting fatigued (for those with large territories)
❏ The gift of gab; a great phone voice
❏ Good people skills (you sometimes have to entertain clients)
❏ Self-motivation and discipline to structure your own work day
❏ Ability to take rejection in stride
❏ Confidence in your abilities and your product (it's tough for even the best to sell merchandise they're not crazy about)
❏ Ability to drink only in moderation, if at all (when entertaining clients)

Physical Requirements

❑ A body that looks trim and fit (particularly if you're selling stylish apparel or equipment you claim to use)

❑ A well-groomed appearance (you're selling yourself as much as the product)

Education

Nothing is needed beyond a high school degree. But some manufacturers prefer those with an associate degree or coursework in business and computers.

Licenses Required

None

Job Outlook

Competition for jobs: very competitive

Getting in is tough, since manufacturers of sports equipment, apparel and footwear often hire from within the sports world rather than looking outside for new applicants. Still, there is high turnover, which means job openings. Most segments of the sports industry are expected to keep growing in the nineties, especially in the areas of personal recreation and fitness, women's sports at the high school and college level and professional baseball, hockey and football.

The Ground Floor

Entry-level job: manufacturer's representative (rep)

On-the-Job Responsibilities

Beginners and experienced reps

❑ Initiate cold calls to potential buyers
❑ Prepare samples (to show buyers)
❑ Set up appointments with buyers
❑ Visit buyers or welcome them to the agency's or manufacturer's office

❏ Promote lines (you may bring along props that the manufacturer provides to "move" the product and educate buyers and their sales clerks or team equipment managers about what makes the product appealing, safe and a good deal)
❏ Demonstrate equipment (or show videotapes that do)
❏ Write up orders and make shipping arrangements
❏ Entertain buyers
❏ Make follow-up phone calls to accounts

◆ **When You'll Work**

Reps work long and erratic hours and have to set aside time for entertaining clients in the evenings and on weekends. Those who sell to teams are busy in the months preceding the season (when large orders are often placed) or after a season ends (so the team is ready for next season). Rush orders may also be placed during the season, when teams suffer unexpected damage to equipment or uniforms and shoes.

Retail sporting goods outlets, clubs and resorts often buy on a year-round basis, although they frequently place orders for particular types of equipment or apparel months before customers are likely to begin looking for them on the shelves. Reps work especially hard during the two major annual trade shows, when buyers come by the thousands to see new product lines.

◆ **Time Off**

Manufacturer's reps take two or three weeks vacation. Those who are employees of manufacturers get the same time off as other employees—often two weeks. Those who are independent take off whatever time they feel they can afford. The slowest times are after Christmas and early fall.

◆ **Perks**

❏ Use of a company car, an expense account, medical benefits (but only for reps on staff)

❏ Merchandise discounts
❏ Free tickets to sporting events
❏ Lots of tax-deductible expenses (for independent reps)

Who's Hiring ◆

❏ Manufacturers of sporting equipment, apparel and footwear
❏ Reps with their own agencies

On-the-Job Hazards ◆

❏ Increased risk of an automobile accident due to frequent car travel
❏ Possibility of stress-related health problems

Places You'll Go ◆

Beginners and experienced reps: frequent opportunity for local or regional travel

The extent of travel varies with the territory. Some reps cover an area within a state, some have entire states and others do regions that include several states.

Reps also travel to the two large annual industry shows: the Super Show, put on by the Sporting Goods Manufacturers Association in Atlanta during the winter, and the World Sports Expo, staged by the National Sporting Goods Association in Chicago during the summer. Reps also attend regional shows throughout the year, as well as seminars, workshops, dealer presentations and association conventions.

Surroundings ◆

Most reps work from their home and spend much of their time on the road, so their surroundings vary with their success: The better they do, the better the motel or hotel they stay in. The type of product you represent also determines your work environment. You may visit college and professional team stadiums and arenas, pro shops and sporting goods stores. With the explosion in high-fashion sports apparel and footwear, some reps also visit department stores and clothing boutiques.

Since entertaining is part of the job, manufacturer's reps can also spend plenty of time at posh resorts and clubs, in the lodge or the pro shop, where they make contacts and deals or close sales. And many sales are concluded after a round of golf or tennis, on a ski run, or riding the chair to the top of the mountain.

Most reps know the inside of their car or airport lounges best.

◆ **Dollars and Cents**

Earnings vary from nothing to a seven-figure salary; the average is $35,000 to $50,000. How much you make depends on your salesmanship, the quality and demand for your line and how "rich" a territory you land. Reps working in far-flung rural areas or states with few big college or professional teams will find it hard to equal the sales of reps in regions where sports teams are concentrated or large metropolitan areas where a variety of buyers are clustered.

◆ **Moving Up**

Success is measured mostly by the number and quality of your lines and, of course, your sales. For more job security and power, you can move "inside"—that is, get promoted to a position as a manufacturer's regional or national sales manager—if you show that you're good at motivating and monitoring others. But many choose to keep their independent lifestyle, even if their incomes are unpredictable.

◆ **Where the Jobs Are**

Reps work countrywide, although the most lucrative territories are in large metropolitan areas with concentrations of retailers and sporting teams, such as New York, Los Angeles, Chicago, Miami, Atlanta, San Francisco, Boston, Dallas, Houston, St. Louis, Minneapolis, San Antonio, Detroit, San Diego, Cleveland and Seattle.

◆ **Training**

Community colleges and the adult education divisions of high schools and universities offer a number of business and computer courses that can be helpful. But learning how to sell is an art that is best developed by doing, not studying. Working for someone in sales or for a rep who is willing to act as a mentor can give you insight and information that coursework cannot.

The Male/Female Equation

◆ Once a male-dominated business, selling for sports manufacturers is now more open to women, especially those who work for apparel and footwear makers, which are often fashion driven. Still, of the 285 agencies represented by an industry trade association, only three are run by women.

Women with some background in golf, tennis or skiing might consider those areas before the more traditionally male sports of football, baseball, basketball and hockey. Among the estimated 3,400 golf reps, about 17 percent are women, according to *Golf* magazine.

Making Your Decision: What to Consider

◆ **The Bad News**

❏ Unpredictable income
❏ Long hours on the road
❏ No benefits if you're an independent
❏ Rejection is built into the job

The Good News

❏ You can run your own show
❏ Flexible hours
❏ Big bucks for the successful
❏ You're plugged into the world of sports or a sport you enjoy

More Information Please

◆ Sporting Goods Agents Association (SGAA)
P.O. Box 998
Morton Grove, Illinois 60053
708-296-3670

Manufacturers' Agents National Association (MANA)
23016 Mill Creek Road, P.O. Box 3467
Laguna Hills, California 92654
714-859-4040

Write or call for a directory of other reps and agencies, listings of job openings, available computer software and tips and guidelines on how to do your job.

Jim Hill, 23,
manufacturer's rep, Founder's Club,
Mission Vejo, California
Years in the business: eight months

How did you become a rep?
I had been a golf pro at a Jack Nicklaus course for four
years. One of the members took a job with Founder's Club,
a golf club manufacturer, and offered me the chance to
triple my salary and get a company car. There seemed to
be more freedom and more money than working as a pro,
so I accepted. Contacts are the way to get a break in the
golf industry.

Do you work exclusively for the company?
Yes. They give me an annual sales quota, and I get a four
percent commission for anything I sell above that. I also
get health benefits, plus life insurance and a car. And a
pension plan may be in my future.

Do you work on the company premises?
No, I am an independent agent and work from home. I
don't have an office at the company, but I do go in quite a
bit because I'm in the area. I have three or four accounts
nearby.

Are there differences in the hours you work as a rep from when you worked as a pro?
On weekends I used to work from 6 A.M. to 4:30 P.M., then wake up the next morning and do it again. Now I have weekends off. I'm not playing as much golf now, and I'm really not into it as much anymore.

What's your territory?
Three counties in southern California, from just under Los Angeles to the Mexican border, including San Diego. My territory will probably do $800,000 this year (1993), but the L.A. County territory, which is handled by a more experienced rep, will probably do $1.7 million.

Describe what you do.
At first I had to go out and make sure I met the people with all 400 accounts. I had to do six or seven a day, and at first it didn't feel as if I was making a dent. Half of the accounts are club pro shops, and only about half of them sell a lot of golf clubs.

About two months into my job, we went "off-course" to all the big golf stores and discount retailers, so that gave me an even bigger territory. That's about 75 percent of my sales now. I still also have my "green grass" accounts, which are golf clubhouses with a driving range or course. They are steady buyers, but most aren't very big.

Describe a typical week.
I always call a week ahead to make an appointment to see an account. I usually see 20 to 25 accounts in a week. I put a lot of mileage on the car, but I'm home most nights.

How long did it take you to feel established?
After I got my first check. But there are times when you get shot down. It took about four months to get really comfortable with my sales pitch, the prices and terms. Talking about how the clubs are built and why they are good clubs is no problem because I've been in golf so long.

What's the best thing about your job?
I love working my own hours, closing a deal and landing a big new account. But if you don't make the sale, there's going to be a guy 30 minutes behind you, trying to sell his clubs.

And I can wake up on Monday morning, throw on a tee shirt and a pair of shorts, and make phone calls for four and a half hours. Then I might be done for the day, and I might have sold $15,000 to $20,000 worth of clubs over the phone. But that's to guys I've done business with before, not the new accounts.

What's the worst part?
Probably the rejection. Driving for six hours and then not making a sale. Driving back home and thinking: What's wrong with this picture? I don't let it lead to self-doubt because you have to bounce back. And credit is a problem right now. With the economy the way it is, there are a lot of places I don't go to anymore because they still owe us money from the last time I was there.

What advice would you give to someone interested in this career?
I'd get out there and meet people in golf or whatever sport you want to rep for. You've got to know the sport and the people in it.

Norine Lassa, 41,
manufacturer's rep,
Norine Lassa and Associates,
Lebanon, New Jersey
Years in the business: 14

How did you break into the field?
My former sister-in-law was a rep in northern California, selling a small line of women's active apparel called Go-belle. The company wanted to take a crack at the New York market, so she told them about me. I had been a secretary on Wall Street for eight years, but I hated my job. They sent me some samples in the mail and told me to go for it.

For the first year, I repped on lunch hours, after work and on weekends. No one taught me how to sell. I just did it.

Did you make mistakes?
Sometimes. Once when I did a presentation, someone asked if it was "SML," which means small, medium and large—

and I didn't know what she meant. I said I'd get back to her on that. Now it's funny, thinking back on it.

I was 26, and it was fun. I was doing some of the trade shows [in New York], and I got to meet some of the other players in women's sporting apparel. They asked me to rep their lines. They were just starting, and I was just starting. So I quit my secretarial job after about a year and seven months of repping. But I didn't make enough money to support myself for the first couple of years.

How long did it take to become established?
A good four years. But now things are different. I hire people who start with me and immediately are making a good income because I have an established territory with established lines.

Do you have a background in sports?
I did competitive swimming, and I was a lifeguard. I'm not a superjock or anything. I just like to sell.

Tell me about your agency.
I represent four companies—Jog Bra, Moving Comfort (women's running, cross-training and walking apparel), Thorlo (athletic socks), and Tyr (swimsuits and equipment). It's an all-female agency with four sales reps, an office manager and myself. When I started selling 14 years ago, this business was male dominated, both in terms of the reps and the manufacturers. Now more and more women are coming in, but we're still a very small portion overall.

What lines did you represent when you got into the business?
Jog Bra was one of them. It was started 15 years ago by two women in Burlington, Vermont. They created a prototype by taking two jock straps, cutting them apart and sewing them back together into a bra. They tested it—and it worked. The prototypes are in the Smithsonian Institute and the Metropolitan Museum.

When I began trying to sell these athletic bras, sports store managers laughed me out of the store or told me to go to lingerie. I pointed out that they were selling jock straps. Now there are nine styles in the Jog Bra line, which is in every sporting goods store in the country. And it's a multimillion-dollar company.

It used to be just the good old boys, selling baseball bats and balls. But that's changed. I've seen retailers become more aware that they need a section in their sporting goods stores for women's apparel.

What do you do as the agency owner?
At this time of year [winter], we're actually showing our new fall line. I call on key accounts only, so I spend most of my time with the Kinneys [Footlocker, Lady Footlocker] and the Herman's of the world. My reps make sure all their retailers know our lines and buy them. The manufacturer pretty much does the rest as far as shipping, billing and credit. My reps also service the retailers, making sure the clerks know the product and giving them ideas on how to promote it.

What territory do you cover?
New York City and its suburbs, New Jersey, eastern Pennsylvania, Maryland, Virginia and Washington, D.C.

Why does anyone who works on commission join an agency such as yours?
Because I have a name and a reputation. Buyers know I make sure my reps are going to do a good job. Plus I train them and work with them. I hope that I bring my expertise to them. I also take them to the shows twice a year and pay their airfare and hotels.

Are you hiring college or noncollege people?
I try to find someone who has some background in the sporting goods industry or who has repped before. I couldn't care less if they have a college degree.

What do you like most about what you're doing?
Probably the networking. I still love selling, but I really enjoy the networking and the relationships I have with my retailers.

What do you like least about your work?
When people don't call a spade a spade. I don't run into too much of that, but you find it in some of these bigger

companies. And it's going through layers of people to get a decision. I'm a doer, and I like answers *now*.

What advice would you give someone who wants to be a rep?
You can't be a really quiet, shy person in sales. The key thing is whether you're self-motivated and disciplined.

If you know where you want to live, find some of the better rep agencies and network with the people who run them. Or go out into the market and see what lines you relate to best.

Dave Hatfield, 41, manufacturer's rep, Crown Sports Sales, Lexington, Kentucky
Years in the business: four

How did you get started?
By mopping floors at my daddy's sporting goods store. There were five of us kids, so we all pitched in. If we didn't have practice after school, we went in to help out, and we worked there during the summers.

It was one of the old-time, full-line sporting goods stores. We had team sales, where you bought all your football, basketball, baseball and soccer equipment. But we also had hunting and fishing stuff. Naturally, we also had retail clothing and did engraving.

Did you work there after you graduated from high school?
I ran it until five years ago. But after two floods and the bad economic conditions in the region, we sold it.

So how did you become a rep?
A rep who used to call on me recommended me to a new agency for the territory. I was 36 at the time, and I was tickled to death when they offered me the job. It was totally different because you're on the other side of the counter.

How was your first year of being a rep?
The lines I was working with were the same I had bought

and used in the store, so I was extremely familiar with the products. I also believed in the products, which helps tremendously. I knew the fit, the quality, and how to write the orders. But I didn't make money right off the bat. One of my lines was from a company that went bankrupt. The first year was a struggle for me financially.

How many lines do you have now?
Six, including helmets, shoulder pads, licensed caps, sleds, travel bags for teams, shirts for coaches and licensed sweatshirts. Our agency works in the Southeast. If a line becomes available through the [trade] association or somebody you know, the head rep will call that manufacturer and try to get it to give us the line in our area.

Do you go to stores or teams?
Both. I call directly on sporting goods stores; that's how we make our money. But we're also involved in the promotional aspect. I went down to the University of Kentucky this morning to talk with the equipment manager and to write his order.

Do you consider yourself a lone eagle?
One of the last. There's no one to hold my hand when things are rough. If I don't get up in the morning and get in my car and see somebody, I don't make any money.

How do you organize your schedule?
We plan our own calendars anywhere from 30 to 45 days ahead, depending on the dealers—how often you have to see them, what their lead time is. You must have a game plan, especially in a big territory. I drive everywhere I go and stay overnight several times a week.

What do you like about the job?
It's the greatest job in the world. You set your own schedule and your own pace. As long as you make sales, the factory is happy with you. And, of course, you get to meet a lot of good people and get to enjoy it to boot.

What are the drawbacks?
Sometimes the numbers they expect you to sell in a territory are unrealistic. Our agency rep in Atlanta has been the number one salesman for Riddell for four years in a row in the helmet and shoulder pad lines we carry. But there are

more high schools that play football in Georgia than there are in my territory (West Virginia and Kentucky). So there is the opportunity to sell more product, which is something manufacturers don't know.

What are you proudest of?
My territory has grown considerably in the four years I've had it, and that makes me happier than anything. It makes me look better in the eyes of the manufacturer and the agency, but it also puts money in my pocket.

Do you have any advice for someone who wants to rep?
You don't have to be a rocket scientist to succeed in this business. If you want to be a manufacturer's rep, try to hook up with good companies and pick lines that do deliver and pay the commission.

Also, know your product and be truthful with your dealers. Let them know they can depend on you. People like to buy from reps they like, reps who give them good service and provide a product that will make them money.

WILL YOU FIT INTO THE SPORTS WORLD?

Before you sign up for a program of study or start to look for one of the jobs described in this book, it's smart to figure out whether that career will be a good fit, given your background, skills and personality. There are several ways to do that. They include:

❑ Talk to people who already work in that field. Find out what they like and don't like about their jobs, what kinds of people their employers hire and what their recommendations are about training. Ask them if there are any books or publications that would be helpful for you to read. Maybe you could even "shadow" them for a day as they go about their duties.

❑ Use a computer to help you identify career options. Some of the most widely used software programs are *Discover,* by the American College Testing Service; *SIGI Plus,* by the Educational Testing Service; and *Career Options,* by Peterson's. Some public libraries make this career software available to library users at little or no cost. The career counseling or guidance office of your high school or local community college is another possibility.

❑ Take a vocational interest test. The most common are the Strong-Campbell Interest Inventory and the Kuder Occupational Interest Survey. High schools and colleges usually offer free testing to students and alumni at their guidance and career-planning offices. Many career counselors in private practice and at community job centers can also give the test and interpret the results.

❑ Talk to a career counselor. Ask friends and colleagues if they know of any good ones, or contact the career information office of the adult education division of a local college; staff and workshop leaders may do one-on-one counseling. The job information services divisions of major libraries sometimes offer low- or no-cost counseling by appointment. Or check the *Yellow Pages* under the heading "Vocational Guidance."

But before you spend time, energy or money doing any of the above, take one or more of the following five quizzes (one for each career discussed in the book). The results can help you decide whether you have the basic traits and abilities that are important to success in that career—in short, whether you are cut out for it.

If becoming a club pro/instructor interests you, take this quiz:

Read each statement, then choose the number 0, 5 or 10. The rating scale below explains what each number means.

> **0** = Disagree
> **5** = Agree somewhat
> **10** = Strongly agree

____I am a talented athlete and would love to teach others my sport

____I stay in shape and enjoy practicing my sport

____I am familiar with the equipment used in my sport and know how to fix and maintain it, and I keep up with new developments

____I know all the rules of my sport or am willing to brush up on them

____I try to keep up with all the latest trends and theories about my sport, and I am interested in current teaching techniques

___I am familiar with the latest fashion trends in apparel and footwear in my sport and would feel comfortable selling them

___I can talk about the complex moves and techniques in my sport in a very basic, clear way to people less familiar with it

___I am easygoing and diplomatic

___I am self-motivated and can work independently

___I am punctual and reliable

Now add up your score. ___Total points

If you scored less than 50, then you probably do not have enough interest in teaching your sport or handling the other responsibilities involved in being a club pro or instructor. If your points totaled between 50 and 75, you may have the necessary passion for your sport, but you may want to brush up on your teaching skills—perhaps through a school or clinic. If you scored 75 points or more, consider yourself a prime candidate for securing a job as a club pro or instructor.

If becoming a sports official interests you, take this quiz:

Read each statement, then choose the number 0, 5 or 10. The rating scale below explains what each number means.

$$0 = \text{Disagree}$$
$$5 = \text{Agree somewhat}$$
$$10 = \text{Strongly agree}$$

___I know the rules of certain sports and the hand signals officials use

___I like the idea of becoming an expert on rules

___I have quick reflexes, good coordination and stamina

___I have a sense of fair play and the flexibility to interpret—not just enforce—the rule book in real game situations

91

___I have confidence in my ability to make the right call and can react quickly and decisively in pressure situations

___I have a thick skin and can take criticism, even abuse

___I have the ability to cool down heated arguments and fights

___I have good communication skills for talking to coaches and players

___I don't let my ego or personal preferences get in the way of my judgment

___I don't mind being anonymous in sports, but I think I can also handle the spotlight with dignity and control

Now add up your score. ___Total points

If your total points were less than 50, you probably do not have sufficient interest or the personality to be a sports official. If you scored between 50 and 75 points, with further investigation and, perhaps, experience calling games, you may do very well as a sports official. If your score was 75 points or more, you have the necessary skills, flair for making calls and love of sports to be a first-rate sports official.

If becoming an equipment manager interests you, take this quiz:

Read each statement, then choose the number 0, 5 or 10. The rating scale below explains what each number means.

$$0 = \text{Disagree}$$
$$5 = \text{Agree somewhat}$$
$$10 = \text{Strongly agree}$$

___I am familiar with the various equipment used in different sports

___I know the rules of a wide variety of sports

___I know or could learn computer basics and math for budgeting

___I can fix and repair various types of sports equipment

___I can be creative and have mechanical aptitude

___I have a knack for keeping track of details and could handle several responsibilities involving different sports at the same time

___I can deal with the stress and pressure of game situations

___I have a thick skin and don't let people upset me

___I am patient and easygoing

___I am punctual and disciplined

Now add up your score.   ___Total points

If your score added up to less than 50 points, chances are you are not cut out for working as an equipment manager. If your total points were between 50 and 75, you probably have what it takes to pursue this career, but you may need to get practical experience to find out if you're really cut out for it. If you scored 75 points or more, you most likely would succeed as an equipment manager.

If becoming a sports photographer or videographer interests you, take this quiz:

Read each statement, then choose the number 0, 5 or 10. The rating scale below explains what each number means.

> **0** = Disagree
> **5** = Agree somewhat
> **10** = Strongly agree

___I have a creative eye for photography and am familiar with camera equipment

___I know how to fix some of my equipment and can improvise when it breaks down

___I understand principles of composition and perspective and of light and the color spectrum as they relate to film or am eager to learn

___I am assertive enough to position myself where I need to be on the field or in an arena to get a great shot

_____I know or would enjoy learning how to work in the darkroom or how to edit tape

_____I know and love sports and can anticipate important plays before they happen and recognize important players and coaches

_____I keep in good shape and can carry heavy equipment

_____I am thick-skinned enough to deal with rejection and rude athletes and coaches

_____I can work under deadline pressure

_____I am willing to try out my skill by working part time or on a freelance basis

Now add up your score.   _____Total points

If you came up with fewer than 50 points, a career as a sports photographer is probably not for you. If your total points were between 50 and 75, you may have what it takes, but you would be wise to put your skills into practice, even if it means shooting the local Little League games. If you scored 75 points or more, you definitely have the personality and skills required of sports photographers, so keep clicking that shutter!

If becoming a manufacturer's rep interests you, take this quiz:

Read each statement, then choose the number 0, 5 or 10. The rating scale below explains what each number means.

> **0** = Disagree
> **5** = Agree somewhat
> **10** = Strongly agree

_____I have some experience in sales or would like to learn about business

_____I would like to learn how sales people develop their pitch

_____I know about the various types of sports equipment, apparel and footwear

___I would not mind spending a lot of my time on the road

___I stay in shape, dress well and enjoy the fashion aspect of sporting apparel and footwear

___I am outgoing and a good conversationalist

___I am disciplined and self-motivated

___I don't mind working on commission, with an uncertain income

___I am confident and can handle rejection

___I have some computer know-how and basic math skills

Now add up your score.   ___Total points

If your total points were less than 50, you probably do not have enough interest in sports fashion apparel and equipment or the personal qualities required to be a successful manufacturer's rep. If your total points were between 50 and 75, you may have an interest in sporting goods but lack some sales pizazz or know-how, both of which can be acquired. If you scored 75 points or more, you're right on track to get a job as a manufacturer's rep.

ABOUT THE AUTHOR

Allen F. Richardson is a freelance writer and photographer. He has written for the *New York Times*, the *Village Voice*, the *SoHo News*, the *Fort-Worth Star Telegram*, *Women's Wear Daily*, *Glamour*, *Mother Jones* and *Life*.

His photographs have appeared on television and in newspapers, magazines and books. He has also served as a consultant to NBC, ABC, CBS, PBS and the BBC and ITN (Britain) news programs, specials and documentaries. He was most recently the London correspondent for *USA Today* and is a columnist for *Touchdown*, a British magazine dedicated to that small but growing group of American football crazies overseas.

Richardson lives in New York with his wife, Karen, and daughter, Samantha. Since the third grade, he has wanted to write a book, as an essay recently unearthed by his mother proves.

This is his first book. It is dedicated, to keep a cherished promise, to his father, Robert F. Richardson, 1925–1984. Thanks, Dad.